Reubin Drisner givdifficult life of homesteaders in western Canada during the late 1920's and onward. Personally, I found the book hard to put down!

Woven into this practical and homespun account is the amazing story of faith, grit and determination of his immigrant parents who came from the Ukraine just prior to the Great Depression to forge a new life with their young family in the vast and rugged land called Canada. In the process, Reubin shares his own personal journey and powerful encounter with the Holy Spirit that laid the ground work for his life of fruitful ministry.

In reading Reubin's book, I was reminded again of an old song than can speak encouragement to each of our hearts, "Little is much when God is in it."

As you read, get ready to believe God for the seemingly impossible in your life!

Paul Willoughby
Former Producer/Host of Nite Lite Live (CTS TV)
Author: *Don't Waste Your Pain –*
The Journey from Brokenness to Wholeness

Newbrook, Calgary-Ogden, Barrhead, Thunder Bay - these are all meaningful locations in the story of Reubin Drisner's life. I have the joy, as I read Pastor Drisner's story, to picture all of these locations as I have been there and they also have meaning for me. *My Life on the Homestead* descriptively details the sacrifice, dedication and simple faith of the Drisner family as immigrants and pioneers. It is a most vivid and witty descriptions of pioneer life.

Those attributes of sacrifice, dedication and simple faith carry on through Reubin's life and ministry as he responds to God's Call, marries Shirley and together they live lives of "builders". No couple defines the builder generation better than the Drisners as they build new churches and parsonages, build up congregations and build the qualities of service and faith into their family, something that continues to this day.

My Life on the Homestead is an inspiring and entertaining read. More importantly it is a necessary reminder of values and qualities that my and future generations can embrace.

Rev. David Wells
General Superintendent
The Pentecostal Assemblies of Canada

Seldom do we think, as we drive down along our well maintained highways, in comfortable vehicles, the laborious price that was paid by previous generations to afford us this convenience. Seldom do we think, as we relax in our comfortable houses, of the incessant, back-breaking toil, of the pioneers, that allowed us to live in this level of ease and style. Seldom do we think of the Fathers and Mothers of faith, who carefully and prayerfully laid a foundation for us, persisting in their belief in the goodness and benevolence of God, in the face of severe hardship and loss.

These stalwarts, trailblazers, designers, inventors, and labourers, who would not quit, are the unsung heroes of our beautiful and bountiful Nation. Their stories must be both told and preserved.

This is a short narrative of the Drisners, a family who endured much, but, with determination lived out the dream of homesteaders. They knew that their sacrifice was essential, both for their own survival, and for the hope of generations yet unborn.

I have had the joy of knowing Reubin Drisner for many years. He is a man I highly respect. I warmly invite you to read this account of his early life. I know that you will be enlightened and encouraged by this story, just as I was.

Rev. Allen G. Downey
Pastoral Care Coordinator
Alberta and Northwest Territories District
The Pentecostal Assemblies of Canada

Should you ever need to be encouraged that God faithfully provides for and sustains the everyday man please pick up Rev. Reubin Drisner's life story. You will have trouble putting it down! Pastor Drisner's account comes from a depth of experience that has been tested through these past 8 decades. Beginning with the account of his ancestry in Eastern Europe we begin to understand how the truth of Psalm 16:6 "the lines have fallen to me in pleasant places, I have a beautiful heritage" is evident today.

In a day when we are rapidly losing men and women of this sterling character, such landmarks must be acknowledged in order for the present generation to understand from whence they came and the potential of what they may yet realize in their own lives.

In reading our brother's autobiography it may seem that his life was filled with many challenges and some hardships. But for him it was a life of great personal satisfaction. He was able to draw upon deep spiritual resources in order to negotiate the arduous tasks of his calling.

What will make the reading of this account so encouraging is the matter of fact manner of telling. The events as written were simply what each day brought.

I am particularly honoured to be able to make these comments as the Drisners were my pastors during part of my university years. I am a witness to the authenticity of this family.

Thank you Reubin Drisner for sharing your life with us in this manner.

Brad Fawcett, B.A., M.L.I.S., M.A.
Vanguard College

Reubin Drisner

MY LIFE ON THE HOMESTEAD
Copyright © 2014 by Reubin Drisner

All rights reserved. Neither this publication nor any part of this publication may be reproduced or transmitted in any form or by any means, electronic or mechanical, including photocopying, recording or any information storage and retrieval system, without permission in writing from the author.

Unless otherwise marked, scripture quotations are from the King James Version, which is in the public domain.

Scripture quotations marked NIV are from THE HOLY BIBLE, NEW INTERNATIONAL VERSION®, NIV® Copyright © 1973, 1978, 1984, 2011 by Biblica, Inc.® Used by permission. All rights reserved worldwide.

Scriptures marked (KJV) are taken from the Holy Bible, King James Version, which is in the public domain.

ISBN: 978-1-4866-0576-7

Word Alive Press
131 Cordite Road, Winnipeg, MB R3W 1S1
www.wordalivepress.ca

Cataloguing in Publication may be obtained through Library and Archives Canada

Dedication

Dedicated first of all to Shirley, my patient, sweet, loving, caring wife, whose companionship I enjoyed for the past sixty years. To our children, John, Sandra, Glenda, Sharon, their spouses and their children who have made our home and family a happy haven. To all our friends who believed in us; encouraged and supported us and enriched our lives with your friendship. My prayer is that this story will inspire others to rise above challenges they are facing and become what God intended them to be.

> *Thou wilt shew me the path of life; in thy presence there is fullness of joy; and at thy right hand there are pleasures for evermore.*
> —Psalm 16:11 (KJV)

Shirley's 80th birthday

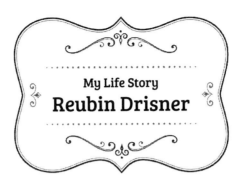

My Life Story
Reubin Drisner

The decision to write my life story began in a discussion of our family roots with Bill and Alice Fawcett over a noon meal at the Sunnyside Seniors' Camp in June 2013. We had known the Fawcetts from our Bible college days in Edmonton in the early 1950s. Our stay in Edmonton was quite brief. Shirley and I entered the ministry with the Pentecostal Assemblies of Canada after graduation, taking us elsewhere, so we never had an occasion to socialize and discuss our roots with the Fawcetts. I was interested in their history and Bill asked me about mine.

Reubin and Shirley – 1953

When our time in the dining room noon was over, Bill said to me, "Reubin, you need to write your life's story. It will be lost if it isn't recorded. You write it and I'll publish it."

"I don't think I am capable of doing that, and I don't think anyone would be interested in reading it."

Bill insisted it was a story worth telling, and he has been encouraging me to get at it. Well, since I really don't have much else to do these days, I might as well take a crack at it. I have nothing to lose and it might be a good exercise for the mind and stave off Alzheimer's disease for a little longer.

My mom and dad, Alvina and Emil Drisner in 1963 at their 40th wedding anniversary

Emil Drisner family and homestead

Me?

Gustav Drisner's second marriage family – 1900
(Michael's younger half siblings and Gustav's second wife)

At the Prince of Peace Manor, where I am now living, one of the residents introduced me to a friend who was visiting her.

"This is my friend Marilyn." (She didn't mention my name.)

Marilyn turned to me. "And who are you?"

"I'm me," came my immediate response.

Thinking about it later I wondered, "Who is 'me'? And, how did I get to be me?"

My parents gave me life. What I have become is the cumulative influences of many things: my DNA, parental guidance and education (or lack thereof), my good or bad choices, such things as community environment and the people of the community. The list is endless. I pondered what made me who and what I am.

To discover myself, I needed to go back and review my life. I decided I should go back to my ancestral roots, as far as I could. Konigsberg, Prussia, where my great grandparents, Gustav and Adelina Drisner, came from. I assume they were farmers there. Sometime in the early 19th century they migrated to Poland. Why, we don't know for sure. We assume it had something to do with the land and farming opportunities in Poland at that time. However, we know why they later left Poland and moved to the Ukraine. Gustav and Adelina had six robust sons and one daughter.

The Ukraine in the 19th century was still a frontier nation that needed people to develop the land. In those days agriculture was the major industry of every nation. Good farmers then, like skilled tradesmen today, were in demand. Farming opportunities in Poland were limited, and Gustav's six sons needed something to do. To prepare land for cultivation in frontier Ukraine would keep six robust boys busy for many years.

Michael Drisner Family – 1912. Emil on far right, back row.

My uncle Asaph told us of the huge piles of trees and shrubs that were piled up and burned in the land clearing process. There were no bulldozers, chainsaws, or tractors. It was all manual back-breaking hard work that required unending commitment. Today we drive through farming communities and admire the fields of golden grain waving in the gentle breeze, but hardly ever think of the lifetime of labour that went into clearing the land of the trees, stumps, roots, and stones by the frontiersmen. This all had to happen before even one bushel of seed could be sown.

Emil and Alvina Drisner

When I visited the Ukraine in 2002, I was told that the farmers of German descent were the best: "They taught us a lot about farming. They had the finest horses and the best equipment and built the best homes and were hard workers."

These qualities were engrained in the DNA, and instilled in the psyche of the descendants. My parents had it, and we inherited it too. That's part of who I am. That's me. We grew up before entitlement was in vogue. We worked from sunrise to sunset every day. There were no days off or weeks of paid vacation. The animals had to be fed and watered daily. We drew the water with a pail attached to a rope over a pulley from the 25-foot hand-dug well. That alone required considerable energy to satisfy the thirst of farm animals that were feeding on dry hay. There were no water taps to turn on.

The manure also had to be removed daily from the barn, and the cows milked twice daily year round. In season, we plowed and sowed the land, cut and stacked the hay to feed the animals in the long cold winters, and harvested the grain. Firewood was cut and split for the cook stove every day, year round. And, during winter, more wood was needed for the barrel heater in the bedroom to keep us from freezing to death. All this made me what I am, and hundreds of others who grew up on homesteads in the Canadian frontiers days.

What a contrast from those days and today. Everywhere we went we most always had a shovel, pitchfork, or axe in our hands. Today we have earplugs in our ears and some texting device in our hands. I wonder which of the two is more conducive to the physical and intellectual development of the person we can be, and eventually could become.

My Family and Home

What do we mean when we speak of family? The term is used for a lot of things. It could be a clan, a tribe, a species, a family of plants. Always it means a common strain, stock, or bloodline—a common ancestry. We were a family of eight, one bloodline and a common ancestry. There, of course, were Dad and Mom (Emil and Alvina); then six children. From eldest to youngest: Adeline, Sefrin, Reinhart, then me, Freda, and Bennard.

We speak of good and dysfunctional families, happy and sad families. What makes a good family? Is it wealth and a beautiful home? A cupboard and refrigerator full of a variety of tasty foods? No work and all play with lots of toys, but no rules? Freedom to come and go and do as one pleases? A closet full of the latest fashions? We had none of these things, yet we were happy.

My Life on the Homestead

Our home was a two-room log house with no insulation. Father had gone from Bruderheim, Alberta, in 1930 to build a log house on the homestead he had acquired for a ten-dollar registration fee.

The homestead was 160 acres of wooded land, eight miles north of Newbrook in northern Alberta. There was no road, not even a trail from Newbrook to the wooded homestead. There was only the Northern Alberta Railways train track. The railway was built in 1914 from Edmonton to Fort McMurray to facilitate the shipping of supplies to the Northwest Territories. Supplies were loaded on barges at Fort McMurray and floated down the Athabasca and Slave rivers, across Great Slave Lake down the MacKenzie River to Inuvik on the Beaufort Sea.

Between the homestead and the railway, which was one mile east, there was a huge swamp near the Alpen Railway Siding. My father went from Bruderheim to build a house for his family on the homestead. From Newbrook he walked four miles down the railroad track to the swamp. From there, he trekked through the bush for another four miles with a saw, an axe, and some food supplies to build a log house for his family on the ten-dollar homestead. The task was not completed before winter.

In the spring of 1931, he loaded all he had on a wagon with a hayrack and left Bruderheim for the homestead with chickens, plow, tools, furniture, and family, with a cow tethered to the wagon. From Newbrook, on their way to the homestead, they drove down the railway tracks for four miles. When they got to the swamp, Dad had to cut a trail through the bush to the homestead, which I believe took about two days. While he was doing that, Mother stayed with the wagon and looked after the livestock and family.

Front of the two-room log house

Back of the two-room log house

    We finally arrived at the unfinished log house that had no door or windows, no shingles on the roof, and just a dirt floor. It showered frequently in those days. I was only two years old, but I remember crawling under the kitchen table to keep from getting wet, protected from the rain by the oilcloth covering the table.

The log house was cold in the winter, hot and fly-infested in the summer, and plagued by mice year round. Sticky flycatchers dangling from the ceiling throughout the house all summer didn't seem to diminish the fly population. Nor could the house cats reduce the mouse population. We just had to learn to live with it. This was a common problem for all homesteader families. We had to remove the telltale marks the mice left behind in the porridge bags or the flour sacks. The flies would sometimes get into the bread dough, and homesteaders didn't know how many well-baked flies they may have eaten. We would at times have to stop eating our soup, and fish a fly out of our bowl, while cooked mice dropping spiced up our porridge.

Another unpleasant irritant was the hordes of mosquitoes that bred in the sloughs and swamps. There was no way to escape these thirsty bloodsuckers. They were the worst in the evening before sundown and before a rainstorm. A white horse would be gray with mosquitoes. The poor animals were terribly tormented by these pests. There were no mosquito repellants in those days. There was only one way to escape these pests and that was by standing in some smoke. Mosquitoes didn't like smoke. We would build a blazing bonfire and then cover it with damp barnyard manure. This created a thick cloud of smudge with an awful stench. The animals would go stand in the smudge for relief. We didn't have screens for the windows or door on the house so the mosquitoes had easy access. We would put some flaming coals in a bucket and some barnyard manure on the fire and place it inside the house. We got rid of the mosquitoes but we then had an awful stench in the house to contend with. The first frost in the fall put an end to those pests, but they always came back the next spring.

It was these hordes of mosquitoes that were a bloodthirsty welcoming committee when we arrived at the unfinished house at the homestead. The amazing thing about the mosquitoes was their ability to draw blood. We go to laboratories where highly trained technicians with hypodermic needles prick us to get blood samples. Sometimes these highly trained technicians have difficulty finding a vein to get a sample. But the mosquito, with its tiny brain and no technical training, never had any difficulty pricking at just the right place and getting their fill.

In the two-room log house, the kitchen was where most of the family interaction took place. It was where the food was prepared and the family came together at meal times. We had only two or three chairs, along with the sloping bench behind the table where we children sat, according to age and size. Before each meal we would all sit while father offered a prayer of thanksgiving.

The kitchen was also a family chapel. After breakfast, Father would read a portion of Scripture and we would all kneel in prayer. It was also the kitchen where we washed up and had our weekly Saturday evening baths in a large galvanized tub. It was where we churned the butter, where we washed our clothes on a scrub board, where the wool from the sheep was spun into yarn on a pedal spinning wheel. It was also here we learned to knit our wool socks and mittens. It was sitting around the kitchen table that we communicated with each other and debated on issues. If there was any spare time, we'd sit at the kitchen table and play a game of Checkers on a homemade board drawn on a piece of cardboard. The kitchen was also the guest room. When we had company drop by, we would visit in the kitchen. There was no chesterfield or reclining chairs in the house. There wouldn't have been room anywhere to put them, even if we could have afforded them.

The most important and useful piece of furniture in the house was the cast iron wood burning stove that stood in one corner of the kitchen. The stove had a firebox on one side and a five-gallon water tank on the other. The top of the stove was used for cooking, but it also had a baking oven. There was a damper on top of the stove, that when closed, would redirect the heat from the firebox to circulate around the oven and not only heat the oven for baking, but also heat the water in the tank. The stovepipe passed through the centre of an enclosed warming closet, about two feet above the stove top, where food could be kept warm before the meal was served. The kitchen stove was very utilitarian. You could have a half-dozen pots cooking or simmering on top at the same time, and be baking bread in the oven and heating water in the water tank. We could also open the oven door slightly and hang our damp stockings or things to dry. On chilly days, you could warm the kitchen by opening the oven door. In the darkness of the evenings, we'd open the firebox door and the sparkling flame would light up the room and we'd spare the cost of fueling the coal oil lamps. Father would often stay up late reading the Bible by the firebox light.

The kitchen stove required constant maintenance. The ashes had to be removed daily from the top and bottom of the oven and firebox, before the fire was lit in the morning. The heat of the stove was regulated not by the turning of a knob, but by adjusting the airflow dampers. In the opposite corner from the stove, next to the table, was a small cupboard where the food supplies and our few dishes were stored.

In the third corner, a stairway led to the attic, which was primarily a place for storage. Such things as bags of flour, the wooden sauerkraut barrel with fermenting cabbage, extra clothes, and hand tools.

The cream separator also occupied some space next to the stairs in the kitchen. For a number of years, the log house and a horse and cow barn were the only buildings on the homestead. So there wasn't anywhere else to store things. We had too much other work to take time out to build a shed or even an outhouse, which was considered a necessity in those days, with last year's Eaton's catalogue for toilet tissue. The paper from the catalogue had to be used sparingly, for it had to last a year until the next catalogue arrived.

On the wall beside the entrance door we had nails to hang our jackets and caps. We never took our shoes off when we came into the house. Actually, we didn't have any shoes to take off. In the winter, we wore felt boots with rubbers which also had to be worn in the house because the floor was cold. In the spring, after the snow had melted, we shed the felt boots and went barefoot all summer. At first, the soles of our feet were very tender and sensitive, but by summer's end the soles of our feet were tougher than any shoe leather and we could walk on rocks and thorns without feeling it.

The entrance to the bedroom from the kitchen was just an opening in the wall with a curtain. The bedroom had two windows: one in the west wall, and the other in the south wall. It was initially furnished with two double beds in the corners of the west wall with the window in between. In front of the window, mother had her Raymond pedal sewing machine, which she frequently used to sew clothes for the girls and patch our bib overalls with material from flour sacks, or any other material she could acquire. There was probably about five feet between the beds. Mother and Father slept in the north bed, and we four children slept in the south bed. Later, when Freda outgrew the cradle, she joined us as well. Three of us slept at one end and two at the other. Besides the two beds and the sewing machine, there was a linen closet in the northeast corner.

Some friends gave us an old Edison windup gramophone with a diamond needle. It was in the opposite corner from the linen closet. The records were real thick and were mostly classical music. The gramophone was the nicest piece of furniture in the house. Years later when father bought a Marconi shortwave battery radio at a farm sale, the gramophone served as a stand for the radio. When we acquired an egg incubator some years later, it also found a spot in the bedroom next to the gramophone.

There was a barrel heater in the middle of the bedroom, a repurposed twenty-five-gallon oil drum. The drum lay on its side and stood on four metal legs about a foot off the floor. A door had been cut out of one end of the barrel so wood could be placed inside and set on fire. At the top of the barrel, on the opposite end from the door, there was an opening for a stove pipe which had a damper on it that controlled the fire inside. When it was extremely cold, the heater had to be red hot to keep the bedroom warm. Because there was no insulation in the ceiling or attic, except for one layer of tar paper, most of the heat escaped through the ceiling. Only the bedroom was heated at night. Everything in the kitchen was frozen stiff by morning, and had to be thawed before we could have breakfast.

Shortly after we arrived at the homestead, Father borrowed money to buy roof shingles and windows. Boards for the dirt floor were also acquired. Dad knew how to mud plaster, so the inside walls of the house were plastered, a task requiring considerable knowledge and skill. First, willow branches were nailed diagonally to the walls, about 3 or 4 inches apart. A pit was dug in the clay dirt near the house. Water, clay, dirt and straw were mixed together in the pit. The mixing was done by bare feet, stomping the straw into the wet clay. When the straw and clay were mixed to the right consistency, Father troweled the mud over the willow branches to make a smooth, even plaster on the wall. After the plaster had dried, a thin coat of sand plaster was applied over the mud plaster. This was later whitewashed, and the walls looked quite nice. I don't know that any of the plaster ever cracked or fell off the walls. The plaster was an insulation on the inside walls. The cracks between the rough logs on the outside of the house were also sealed with mud plaster to keep the winter cold out. However, the summer rains washed the outside plaster out of the cracks and they had to be redone every fall before winter. The outside of the house was not painted.

Preparing mud for plastering.

About a dozen feet from the house door, the hand-dug well was our water supply for the house and the barnyard animals, but was also a cooler for cream, meat, and butter, which we put in a bucket on a rope and lowered into the well to be kept from spoiling during the hot summer months. The large vegetable garden surrounded the house on the north and east side. In front of the bedroom and kitchen windows, Mother made some circular flowerbeds with a vibrant array of flowers. Mother also planted a variety of colourful flowers on both sides of the long path that went through the garden from the house to the roadway. The flowerbeds and the flower-lined path brightened up an otherwise drab environment, at least for the summer. There were no flower seeds to be bought in the store, or perhaps it was that there was no money to buy seeds, so Mother always harvested the ripe seeds in the fall for next spring's planting. It was our job to hand-weed the vegetable garden. We didn't have time to do this while we were going to school. By the time the school closed at the end of June for the summer break, the weeds had taken over. We spent weeks carefully weeding the garden so as not to disturb the planted vegetables. Besides weeding the garden, we spent most of the summer break picking wild berries in the fields, swamps, and bush, which mother preserved in jars to be eaten over the long winter months.

The house also had two cellars: one under the kitchen, and the other under the bedroom floor, both accessed by trap door. The cellars had to be under the house to protect the contents from the winter frost. The kitchen cellar was where we kept all the jars of preserves, pickles, fruit, and meat, while the bedroom cellar held potatoes and other vegetables. Potatoes were a dietary staple on the homestead. Mother had dozens of ways to serve potatoes. There were potato perogies, soup, boiled, baked and fried potatoes, potato pancakes, and potatoes in the form of a cake baked in the oven. I don't know what all the ingredients for the potato cakes were, but I think it was probably potatoes, flour, eggs, and bacon. They were delicious with Rogers Golden Syrup or sour cream. We would fill the bedroom cellar with potatoes when we dug them up in the fall. By spring, about two thirds were used up, and the remaining potatoes in the cellar would begin to sprout. We children had the task to go down into the dark, damp, smelly cellar and remove the sprouts from all the potatoes. Otherwise, the potatoes would soon begin to decay. This was a detestable task, but our life depended on those potatoes till the new crops were ready to be eaten.

The house on the homestead had no electricity, water taps, or central heating. There was no room for any privacy. We certainly wouldn't expect anyone to live like that today. Why did they do it then? Did everyone in Canada live like that?

Homesteading Was Not a Choice!

Why would anyone in their right mind choose to be a homesteader, and move his family into the bush miles from the nearest town, to live in dire poverty, and work from dawn to dusk every day of the year to eke out a living? Besides that, there was no guarantee of success. The challenges the homesteaders faced seemed at times insurmountable. They were on their own, with no one there to help. No government funding or assistance. It was sink or swim. If you didn't succeed, or perished, others would follow and try where you failed. Why did Emil Drisner take his wife and family to live in the bush, in this harsh environment in northern Alberta? Did he do it in ignorance? No.

Emil grew up on a farm in the Ukraine. His father Michael, the second eldest son of Gustav and Teresa Drisner, was both a pastor in the local Baptist church and a farmer. The Baptist pastors at that time didn't receive a salary from the church and had to support themselves and provide for their families' needs. Every farmer had to be independently self-sufficient. They had to have cows for milk, cream, butter, and cheese. They had sheep for wool, chickens for eggs, geese for their feathers to make quilts, pigs for bacon, horses to do the field work. They had fields of wheat and rye for bread, coarse grains to feed the animals, flax to weave into clothes, fruit trees for fruit, and a big garden for vegetables.

My Father, Emil, was the youngest of three sons in Michael and Teresa's family. Emil's two older brothers had gone to the United States before World War I. (As well, Jacob Drisner, Gustva and Adelina's oldest son and Michael's brother, was farming in North Dakota.) So Emil, the only son still at home, had to do most of the farm work. Yes, Emil knew very well what challenges he was going to face on the homestead. As a matter of fact, farming was the only trade he had learned. He knew how to plow the field and sow the seeds. He knew how to use the scythe to cut hay and grain, and how to thrash the grain with a flail. He knew how to build a log house, how to make firewood for the cook stove and barrel heaters, and how to care for the farm animals. Yes, Emil was prepared to meet the challenges of homesteading in Canada. Why did they choose Canada? Why not Argentina or some other country with a more temperate climate?

From Cold Siberia to Cold Canada

How did these successful German farmers in the Ukraine end up in Siberia? Everything was going so well for them in the Ukraine. The farm was well established and productive. The church was also doing well and Pastor Michael was much loved, so we have been told. The future appeared to hold nothing but blissful contentment.

All of this changed very abruptly.

On June 28, 1914, Austria's Archduke Franz Ferdinand and his wife Sophia were assassinated by the Yugoslav nationalist Gavrilo Princip. This triggered the beginning of World War I on July 28, 1914. This war raged on for four years. What did all this have to do with Siberia, and Emil Drisner homesteading in Canada, Northern Alberta?

When Germany declared war on Russia in the spring of 1915, and began their advance into the Ukraine, the Russians were afraid that the large German population in the Ukraine might join forces with the oncoming German army. For security reasons, they decided to disperse the German people far into the interior of Russia. Many were dispersed to the Volga Valley, and others sent to other regions in Russia. Michael Drisner and his family lived, at the time, in the German community of Lesowschtschisna. The police came and informed the people that in ten days they had to be prepared to leave. They told them that they could only take what they could carry; or if they had a team of horses and a wagon, what they could load on the wagon. It was just before harvest. They had to dispose of or leave everything behind, including the ripe crops for others to harvest.

In ten days the police did come and began to herd the whole community of Germans away. They didn't know where they were being taken, but for six weeks the police herded them about thirty kilometers each day. Every day some of elderly and the weak died. At the end of every day, shallow graves were hurriedly dug by the roadside to bury those who had died. For the night, they camped out in the open. There were no Holiday Inns with freshly washed sheets, neatly tucked over Posturepedic mattresses. There were no golden arches, fast food outlets with tasty burgers at the end of the day. After six weeks of marching, the German people were then loaded into train boxcars like animals and for two weeks were transported to Samara, Siberia, near the Ural Mountains. On the train, due to the crowded conditions with no provision for personal hygiene, people became desperately ill and some more died. Freda, an infant cousin of ours, became ill and a few months later died in Siberia.

When they finally arrived at their destination in Siberia, they were put in a stockade for a brief time and then released into the community without any assistance or any provisions by the government. This region was inhabited by the Tartar people who were of Mongolian descent. Historians do not seem to agree for certainty where they initially came from and how they got there. It is estimated that at one time there were about ten million Tartars spread over a vast region from Mongolia to all of Eastern Europe. Some say they came with Kublai Khan, the famous warrior who invaded Russia in the 12th Century. They spoke a strange language, Buryat, and they were devout Muslims. Their culture and language was altogether foreign to the weary, exhausted German Baptists from the Ukraine. The influx of a trainload of people in this Tartar community severely strained the resources needed to provide the necessities of life for their citizens. This was stressful for not only the Germans, but also for the local inhabitants. There was no employment available, and every household had in store only enough food for their family. There were no transport trucks, in those horse and wagon days, bringing food supplies from other regions and faraway places. There would be no additional food until the gardens and crops would be harvested next year. In today's marketplace we can buy, year-round, food from nations around the world. In Samara Siberia, at the beginning of the 20th Century, if they didn't grow it or produce it, then they didn't have it.

For nearly 400 years Russia was ruled by the Romonov family tzars. During their reign, Russia was mostly a nation of rich landlords and poor serfs. The serfs were owned by the landlords and were treated badly. In 1917 the serfs revolted demanding changes. There were two factions to the civil war in Russia: those who were against changes and were known as the Whites and were supported by the tzar, and those who demanded changes and promised the serfs freedom and ownership of the land, and were known as the Red Bolsheviks. Lenin arranged for the execution of the tzar and his entire family. The nation of Russia was then without any leadership. The Whites, who were against any change, were led by Alexander Kolchak; the leader of the Red Bolsheviks was Lenin who wanted things to change. This war raged for four years. In trying to seize control of Russia, Lenin chose Throsky, a brilliant leader, as his war general. Trosky enticed army recruits to join the Red Revolutionary Army with the promise that the army would always be fed first and the civilians would have to live on what was left over. After the appropriation of food for the troops there was little left for the citizens and nothing for the despised Germans. In the four-year conflict, over 800,000 soldiers perished and it is estimated that another ten million citizens died of malnutrition. My grandmother and grandfather were two of the ten million. Lenin who became the indisputable leader of the Red Bolsheviks, defeated the Whites and became the first premier of Russia. Lenin died in 1924 and Joseph Stalin became the new premier.

During the four-year conflict, 1917–1921, the Michael Drisner family was given a large room in a mansion in Siberia in which to live. The mansion had been owned by a rich baron before the revolution. The rich baron, after his estate was taken from him, was probably put in prison or sent to a concentration labor camp where he would have been worked to death. The room in the mansion had a fireplace where they cooked their meals. This mansion was also used as a morgue during the war. Every morning there was a pile of corpses on the doorstep of the mansion. The bodies were brought into a separate room in the mansion where they were placed in coffins in preparation for burial. My father, eighteen years of age, was conscripted as a gravedigger for the duration. Many years later, at Newbrook, when one of the elderly members of the church had died they asked my father to help dig the grave. My father refused. He said that he had dug so many graves in Siberia, he just could not do it. Apparently, it would have brought back too many bad memories.

At the end of the civil war, the German families were finally given permission to return to the Ukraine. Samara was about 3,000 kilometers from Lesowschtschisna, Ukraine. My family bought a team of horses and a wagon. They loaded their few belongings in the wagon and set out on the long journey back to the Ukraine. Teresa had already died of malnutrition, so it was Michael; his three daughters: Lydia, Ida and Adina; my father, Emil; and two grandchildren Arnold and Meta, Aunt Lydia's children. Ida was my father's twin sister, who had married Mr. Renz, another dispersed German in Siberia, and he too came with them on their return journey.

They began their journey in June of 1921. Their food supply was soon exhausted, and they had to abandon the horses and wagon because they didn't have any feed for the horses. They then tried to hop on moving trains to reach their destination. Lydia slipped and fell, and the train wheel ran over her foot and cut off two of her toes. Lydia ended up in the hospital.

My father stayed behind to look after Lydia's two children, Meta and Arnold, his niece and nephew who were about eight and ten, while their mother was in the hospital. The rest of the family continued on back to the Ukraine. While Lydia was in the hospital, Emil raided gardens for food, for himself and his niece and nephew. At night they slept in nearby haystacks. One day, my father, in search for something to eat, came upon an army camp. Food was being dished out to the soldiers who stood in line. Emil stood and observed what was going on.

Each soldier had a container and the person dishing out the food asked each soldier, "For how many?" and he received the food and went on his way.

My father was wearing a soldier's uniform that he had acquired somewhere. Perhaps it had belonged to one of the dead soldiers he had dug a grave for. He hurriedly got a container and got in line. He was asked the same question, "How many?"

Dad stated the number and got the food. At least they ate well that day.

After a two-week stay in the hospital, Lydia was released. Her doctor was a compassionate man, and he made arrangements for her, her two children, and Emil to acquire tickets on the train the rest of the way back to the Ukraine. When they arrived at the train station and were prepared to board, a policeman with a gun pushed them aside and would not allow them to get on the train. The train was soon filled with uniformed soldiers and there was no room for them. Then, there was a freight train with some soldiers in a boxcar. They got into it, but the soldiers did not want them in the car with them, and made them get off. Then they found a train car full of refugees, and asked if they could ride with them.

They said, "We bought this car and there isn't any room for anyone else."

One kindhearted woman spoke up, and said that she was willing to share her space with them, and they were allowed on the train.

When they arrive at Kursk, they had to get off and take another train that would take them to the Ukraine. This train was a passenger train and they made the rest of the journey in comfort and luxury. They arrived at their home in Lesowschtschisna in October. That journey, from Siberia to the Ukraine, took them four months from June to October.

Upon their arrival, they learned that Michael had died on the journey. Michael would have been in his early to mid-fifties. His early death was probably largely due to malnutrition and exhaustion. They found that their home had been vandalized during their absence. The fruit trees had all been cut down for firewood. All they had left behind when they were forced to leave was gone. The communist government had taken over the land. They had come back with nothing, to nothing.

Lydia was able to contact her husband, Gus, who by then was on the police force in Racine, Wisconsin, U.S.A. Lydia Kelm and her two children were able to immigrate to the United States, to be with Gus Kelm. Ida, Emil's twin sister and her husband, established their own home in the Ukraine. Emil and his teenage sister Adina had no one and nowhere to live.

Romance and Marriage Without Finance

Emil was a rather handsome, good-natured dude in his early twenties. He got his eyes on a beautiful young lady, the local blacksmith's daughter, Alvina Hein. She was the eldest sibling in the Hein family. She had two brothers, and four younger sisters. The Hein family attended the same Baptist church as Emil and Adina. It was the custom in those days that suitors didn't make a proposal of marriage to a lady. The request for consent to marry was made by a matchmaker to the father of the young lady. Alvina had other suitors who had come to court her in luxurious chariots and fine horses, but she was not interested in them. Then there was Emil Drisner, who had nothing. He came in bare feet and tattered clothes to see Alvina. He did not have a home or a family, but he loved Alvina and she loved him. Emil had a matchmaker go and speak to Julius Hein, Alvina's father, of his intentions and to ask for permission to marry Alvina. Alvina, of course, would have the final say. When Julius, the successful blacksmith, consulted his daughter and discovered that she loved this poverty-stricken, barefooted young man he tried to dissuade her.

He pointed out the obvious. "He doesn't have anything! He doesn't have a trade! He doesn't even have a family! The man has nothing! Look at his bare feet and tattered clothes! How is he going to support you? How are you going to live?"

Alvina said, "But Father, he is a Christian, and he loves God. And Father, I love him and I want to marry him." And she did.

They began their married life and family in the Ukraine. I don't know where they lived after they were married, but probably in the vandalized house. It was Alvina who insisted that they leave the Ukraine and move to the U.S.A.

She told our father, "There is no future here for us or our children since the communists have taken over."

Their first choice was the U.S.A, as this was where Emil's two brothers August and Asaph, his sister Lydia's husband, and Emil's Uncle Jacob were already living. However, the United States' borders were closed to immigrants from Eastern Europe. Aunt Lydia and her two children had been allowed in because Lydia's husband was already in the States. There was one other possibility to get out of the Ukraine, and that was Emil's cousin, Daniel, who had immigrated to Canada before World War I.

They got in touch with Daniel in Bruderheim, Alberta, and asked him to sponsor them. Daniel was financially able and happy to sponsor them. My mother and father sold the few belongings they had, and prepared to sail to Canada on board the ship, Empress of France, at the port in Odessa on the Black Sea. They spent their last few days in the Ukraine in the courtyard of Julius Hein's blacksmith shop. The courtyard had housing for the employees that worked at the shop, and Emil and Alvina were staying in one of these houses.

The night before they were going to leave, some bandits came into the house through an open window where they were sleeping. They, of course, awakened my father and the rest that were sleeping there, and grabbed Emil by the throat and demanded their money. Emil said that he did not have any money.

They said, "We know you have money, and if you don't give it to us we'll kill you." The racket awakened the other employees at the blacksmith shop compound, so they came running with clubs of wood and banged on the door demanding to know what was going on. The bandits became frightened and made a hasty exit by climbing over the table and back out the window. The money the bandits were demanding, along with their tickets, was in a can beneath the table they crawled over to enter and escape.

In early fall of 1927, Emil and Alvina along with their two small children Adeline (age two and a half) and Sefrin (age one), boarded the Empress of France. After two weeks at sea they arrived at Montreal, Quebec, Canada. There, they boarded the train for a long ride to Bruderheim, Alberta. My father recalled, "On that long train ride from Montreal we saw nothing but bush and rocks. I wondered to what kind of country we had come? How can anyone grow anything on these rocks and in these trees?"

They arrived in Bruderheim in early October 1927. The worldwide depression came in 1929. For two years my father was able to find employment, and they rented an abandoned farmhouse in the country about five miles north of town. They planted a garden and bought a cow for milk and some chickens for eggs, a team of horses and wagon for transportation. When there was no work to be found due to the depression, and they were unable to pay the rent, the owner of the property told them they could not live there if they could not pay. So, what could they possibly do? They were told there was still land available in the north.

For a ten-dollar registration fee, they could get a quarter section of land, 160 acres. My father must have gone to Newbrook, sixty miles north of Bruderheim, to see what was available. Homesteaders had already come to Boyle and Ellscott, fifteen to thirty miles north of Newbrook, by way of Athabasca, and had taken up most of the land in that region. There was still some land available between Ellscott and Newbrook. This area was a swampy, muskeg region, not considered suitable for farming. Dad found a quarter of land located on high ground covered with trees. The trees were big and the grass was tall. He thought surely this must be good land. It had all that he knew that they would need to survive. So Dad borrowed ten dollars and acquired the 160 acres of bush, eight miles north of Newbrook. Homesteading was not a choice, it was survival.

I was born in the Lamont hospital on July 10, 1929, and for over twenty years I worked alongside the rest of the family to make the homestead a comfortable and profitable place to live.

Somebody observed that life was indeed hard in Canada, and most of the rest of the world, during the ten years of the Great Depression. The homesteaders probably fared better than the urban dwellers. The homesteader, living in log houses in the woods, did not have some of the luxuries of the city dwellers. However, the vegetable garden, the cows in the barn, the hens in the henhouse, the berries in the woods, and the grain in the field produced wholesome food. The trees provided heat for the house and fuel for the cook stove. The homesteaders had nothing, but they had everything they needed to survive.

Somebody said: *"The happiest people don't necessarily have the best of everything; they just make the best of everything they have."*

Life on the Homestead

Apart from the First Nations, Canada has always been a nation of immigrants. Canada became a nation at the time of Confederation in 1867 with a population of 3.5 million people. Most of the population lived in the east: Southern Ontario, Quebec, and the Maritime provinces. The Northwest region of Canada was a vast wilderness populated by 15,000 Métis and an unknown number of First Nations people. Immigrants were needed to populate this vast region. The government enticed immigrants to come from the U.S.A and Europe by offering free land. In 1905, when Alberta and Saskatchewan became provinces in the Northwest region, 150 thousand immigrants came looking for free land. The southern parts of the Prairie Provinces were treeless. All that was required was to turn over the sod with a plow and sow the seeds and watch it grow to reap a harvest. The northern regions were forested, with huge trees that had to be removed before a plow could be put to the soil or any seeds sown.

Other than the forests of trees, there were many large and small swamps in the northern regions of the Prairie Provinces. Initially, all the territory north of the North Saskatchewan River was considered unsuitable for agriculture, and it was said that families would not be able to sustain themselves in this region. However, immigrants kept coming expecting to get free land. The only solution was to see if the north could work. So in 1908, the Federal Department of the Interior commissioned Frank Crean, a civil engineer, to assess the agricultural capabilities of Northwest Saskatchewan and Northeastern Alberta. Crean reported that there was much fertile land in this region and that cereal crops could be grown there. The region was then surveyed and made available to be farmed. The quarter of land that Emil registered, and paid the borrowed ten dollars for, was in this region.

Since the homesteaders didn't have any power equipment, everything had to be done by hand. After years of ceaseless toiling, they only had a few acres and a garden plot under cultivation.

When Emil and Alvina arrived in Canada in 1927 they were penniless. The worldwide depression of 1929, which lasted for at least one decade, made it impossible for immigrants to get work. Their only option was to acquire a homestead—a place where they could build a log house, acquire a cow or two for milk, cream, and butter, some chickens for eggs, plant a garden for vegetables, and pick wild berries for fruit.

Many of the homesteaders were bachelors, and their houses were one-room structures. Emil built a two-room house for his family.

The homesteaders would find employment at harvest time and other odd jobs to earn a few dollars to buy other necessities such as clothing, sugar, and salt. At harvest each year, Emil would go to Bruderheim for about two months to work in the harvest fields. Alvina stayed on the homestead and looked after the children and animals. We also had a small income from cream cheques. Cream cheques were the money we received for the extra cream we shipped in cream cans to the creameries either in Edmonton or Lac La Biche. Our dairy herd gradually increased from one cow to a dozen and finally to over twenty cows. By then, with the extra income, we were able to buy farm equipment and build additional barns to house the animals and chickens.

I asked someone if they knew how to milk a cow. They said, "No! How does one milk a cow?"

Well, first of all you have to find the cow. The first thing we did in the morning, and the last thing at the end of the day, was to go out to the pasture to find the cows to bring them home so we could milk them. The cows could be anywhere on 300 acres of bush pasture. They might be lying down hidden from view in a grove of willows contentedly chewing their cud. There was always a lead cow in every herd that would determine where the herd would graze in the pasture. We put a cowbell on a leather strap around the neck of the lead cow. The bell would ring when the cow was grazing or walking. We would listen for the ring of the bell to determine where in the wooded pasture the cows might be. If the cow was lying down chewing her cud, the bell would not ring, and we would have to wander through the bush in search of the cows.

We always had dogs on the farm. We taught the dogs to nip the heels of the cows if they were lagging behind or hiding in the bushes. The dog would go after them and they would hasten to join the other cows on their way to the farmyard where we did the milking. Now, we had to stay on friendly terms with the cows, so the cows did not know that the dogs were nipping their heels at our command. The cows had a choice to give or withhold the milk. So we had to speak kindly to the cows and pat them gently so they would not withhold their milk or kick us when we tried to milk them. When you were on friendly terms with a cow, she would stand still anywhere and let you milk her.

To milk a cow, you would need a milk stool and a milk pail. The cow's udder was at the rear end where the tail is. The tail was the cow's fly and mosquito swatter. So while you were milking, you were being swatted. This was not really a problem, except when the cow's tail was wet and dirty.

You would seat yourself next to the udder on the milk stool, and then put the milk pail between your knees and hold it firmly there by tightly squeezing the milk pail. You could not set the pail on the ground because the cow might lift her back leg to scratch an itch or brush off a horse fly that was biting her, and her leg would end up in the milk pail, spilling or spoiling the milk.

Every cow's udder has four dispensers called teats. Before you begin milking, you have to gently massage the udder so the milk will be released to flow to the teats. You take the teat in your hand and squeeze it from the top down. An experienced milker uses both hands on two teats, rhythmically alternating the squeezing between the left and right hands. On average, the cows would give three to four gallons of milk a day, or one and a half to two gallons per milking. It takes about ten to fifteen minutes to milk a cow by hand.

The most cows I ever milked at one milking was twelve. I do not remember why I did not go to church with the family this one Sunday, but I was home alone. The church usually only had one service from one to three in the afternoon. We would arrive home before supper, in time for the evening chores. We were milking twelve cows by hand at the time and there were usually three or four milkers on hand to do it. When the family was late getting home that Sunday evening, I rounded up the cows and started milking, thinking they would surely be home shortly to help me finish. But, they did not arrive. After an hour or so, I began to worry, thinking that the rapture had taken place and I was left behind because I had not gone to church. As I was milking the last cow, I was relieved to see them drive up and inform me that there was a guest speaker at the church and they had a second service. Sometime later, we bought a milking machine and increased the herd to over twenty cows with one person doing the milking without any difficulty.

Pulling down trees to prepare land for cultivating

We three eldest sons were able to help with the work on the farm: fencing, clearing land for cultivation, making hay for winter feed and, of course, the endless daily chores. The girls, Adeline and Freda, could help mother with housework. After the mid-1930s, things began to get better. Not only did we have cream cheques, but we boys were pretty good with the .22 rifle we owned. There was an abundance of squirrels and rabbits that we would shoot and skin. We had to stretch the hides on boards and let them dry before we shipped them to Winnipeg, Manitoba. I don't remember how much we were paid for these hides. I think for a rabbit hide in good condition we received five or ten cents. The squirrel hides were worth quite a bit more. We also shot prairie chickens and ducks, which thrived in the area. The meat we brought home for the dinner table also helped with the family budget.

Making hay at Cash Lake

When we were old enough to work out, we would bring the money we earned and put it with the other farm funds to pay for things that were needed. Reinhart and Sefrin (Sef for short) felled trees one winter for Andy Ellison, who had a sawmill in the bush northeast of Lesser Slave Lake. They were paid a certain amount for each tree they felled and de-limbed.

In the fall of 1949, I went with Lawrence Ellison, Andy Ellison's nephew, to set up his bush sawmill camp south of Hondo. To get to the campsite, we had to cross a wide swamp with a bulldozer pulling a stone boat loaded with supplies. The caterpillar bulldozer kept breaking through the muskeg and getting stuck because the swamp wasn't frozen yet. Then we had to find a well-rooted tree to fasten the caterpillar winch cable to and winch the caterpillar out of the swamp. It took us all day to cross the swamp and get to the campsite.

The campsite needed a cookhouse and dining room, dormitories for the sawmill workers, and housing for the cook and kitchen staff. The two sawmills had to be set up. The trees that were felled in the bush had to be brought to the mill site. They were first dragged by a small caterpillar tractor to a tree collecting site, and dragged from there by a truck with a winch to the sawmill site. At the sawmill site they had to be cut into various lengths to be ripped into lumber. At the mill site, they had what was called a Suicide Saw. It was a large circular saw mounted on two wheels powered by an air-cooled engine. There were no safety guards around the high-speed circular saw blade. If one stumbled and fell on the blade, it would mean instant and certain death, hence the name. When the mill became operational, I was first given the job to operate the Suicide Saw.

Bush work was a hard and dangerous job. Trees were felled by a two-man crosscut saw. They didn't have chainsaws back then. The trees did not always fall the way the fellers expected them to fall. The fellers had to not only look out for themselves, but for other fellers in that location. That winter, one feller was struck by an unexpected deadwood tree. He lay unconscious in the bush in minus-forty-degree weather until they were able to bring him into camp on the back of a flatbed truck. They wanted to put him in a car and take him to the nearest hospital, fifty miles away in Athabasca. There were only a few cars at the camp and none of them could be started because of the cold. They finally got one started, but it was too late. The wounded man died on the way to the hospital. His life might have been saved had he been wearing a hard hat.

After a while, I was given the best job in the camp. The lumber had to be hauled from camp to Hondo, about twelve miles over frozen swamp. From there it was shipped by train to retailers. The lumber from the sawmill was loaded directly onto huge sleighs. A gravel truck with a hitch and tire chains was used to pull the loaded sleighs to the railroad station at Hondo. I was asked to drive this truck. It was an older truck, but it was warm and easy work to pull the loaded sleighs to Hondo and bring the empty ones back. The truck's transmission began to growl, so I was told to check the oil level in the transmission. To do that, one had to crawl under the truck and unscrew a plug on the side of the transmission. I did that and there was no oil at the plug level. I stuck my finger in the hole to see if I could feel any oil. When I tried to withdraw my finger, the skin doubled up, and I could not get my finger out. It was a very cold day and the transmission was cold. I was stuck under the truck. I called for help. Help came, but they could not get my finger out. So they had to unbolt the transmission from the truck to free me. By then my finger was badly frozen and I had to go to the hospital for medical treatment. I went on compensation for a month or so, and have had to live with a deformed finger for the past sixty-five years. That incident ended my career as a woodsman lumberjack.

Our Life on the Homestead

I was the first of the six children to be born in a hospital. Adeline, Sefrin, and Reinhart were all home births. Reinhart was born on March 9, 1928. Upon their arrival in Canada in October 1927, Mother was four months into this pregnancy.

At birth, Reinhart did not start to breathe and those in attendance gave him up as dead. Our father, being a man of prayer, took Reinhart in his arms and prayed that God would give this baby life and Reinhart began to breathe. I came into the family sixteen months later, born on July 10, 1929, at the Lamont hospital. I was considered the first "all Canadian Drisner." Adeline and Sefrin were home births born in the Ukraine. Adeline was seven years old, Sefrin five, Reinhart three, and I was nearly two when we arrived at the homestead. Freda and Bennard were born in the Radway hospital in 1933 and 1938, after we had moved to the homestead in 1931.

The six Drisner siblings at church.

They tell me that at birth I was one of the homeliest, skinniest babies they had ever seen. When I was just a few weeks old, the pastor of the Moravian Church in Bruderheim came to visit my mother. He apparently took me in his arms and prayed for this homely baby and prophesied that God was going to use me in ministry. I wonder if it was my homeliness that prompted this prophetic utterance, or if it was an anointed insight from God. Perhaps the compassionate pastor felt that with my looks my only options would be the ministry. My mother, being a staid Baptist, probably did not put too much stock in this Moravian pastor's prophecy. Though I do recall, when I was still quite young, her telling someone what the Moravian pastor had prophesied over me. She never spoke to me about this. She had too many other things to occupy her mind than to think of things that might transpire at some time in the distant future.

Our mother, Alvina, was an exceptional woman. She was a great, loving, caring mother and homemaker. She also had prodigious organizational skills, which she had developed in her youth in the Ukraine, assisting her father, the blacksmith. She went with him to the city of Zhitomir to buy all the supplies needed for the blacksmith shop. I assume she may also have helped her father in the management of the shop. Mother pretty well managed the homestead, not in a domineering way but in a gentle, knowledgeable way. Everything was always discussed and decisions were made by consensus. We all worked together as a team. The homestead was run like a well-oiled machine with Alvina as the chief engineer. With Father so often away working somewhere or delivering sleigh loads of tamarack fence posts sixty miles to Bruderheim in the winter to make a few extra dollars, Mother had to run the homestead. Tamarack trees grew on the nearby swampy regions and made good fence posts, because it was hard wood and did not rot like other trees. It was hard work in the cold winter, after the swamps were frozen, to cut the trees and then haul them in the cold winter those sixty miles to make a few dollars.

Our father was a skilled, hard worker and was often away mud plastering and working elsewhere to earn a little money. Later he got work in the Swift's meatpacking plant in Edmonton. Mother was left alone to look after things with the children. Looking back, I am amazed at how well we managed with so little. Someone said, "An ounce of mother is of more worth than a pound of preacher." Mother didn't preach, but she made us aware of what needed to be done and expected us and trusted us to do it.

Father could read German but had never learned to write. When he was working in Edmonton he had his German landlady, where he lived, write a letter to Mother for him. After the letter was written and ready to be mailed, Father asked the landlady where he had to go to mail the letter. She told him to go down the street to a red box and put the letter in the box and the mailman would pick it up. My father went down the street and came to a red box on a pole. He examined the box but couldn't figure out how to put the letter in this box. Soon a big red truck with a screaming siren and flashing lights came directly to where my father was. The firemen asked him what he was doing. My father in his limited broken English explained to them that he was trying to mail a letter to his wife. That he had been told to go down the street and put it in the red box. The fireman pointed to the red mailbox farther down the street and took the letter from my father and mailed it for him. I'm sure the firemen must have shaken their heads and thought that my father was just another ignorant immigrant. Mother was happy to receive the letter and knew nothing of the mailbox incident until Father came home.

Our father, Emil, had an even, carefree disposition. He was everybody's friend. He spoke to everyone: neighbour, acquaintance, or stranger. When driving down the road, he would meet someone travelling the opposite direction, and always stopped to have a short visit. Our horses got so used to this habit that they would stop whenever we were passing someone, even when our father was not on the wagon. When our parents retired from the homestead and took up residence in Edmonton, our father would frequently ride the city bus or street car. He would come home and tell the family the life stories of the people he sat with on the bus. People felt comfortable with him and would confide in him and unburden their hearts to him.

Our father, who had not gone to school a day in his life, spoke five different languages. So he was able to communicate with most of the immigrants in our neighbourhood. He often used this skill to his advantage. One day he was caught jaywalking on a busy street in downtown Edmonton. A policeman stopped him, started to give him a tongue lashing, and wanted to fine him. Father shrugged his shoulders and pretended he did not know what he was saying, and spoke to the policeman in another language, possibly Buryat, the language of the Tartar people. The policeman gave up in frustration and let him go.

Father was a peaceful man and a peacemaker. Our homestead community was made up mostly of immigrants from Eastern Europe. At the beginning of World War II, when the German army invaded Eastern Europe, intense hatred of anyone German was prevalent. My father was in the local store one day where a number of Slavic-speaking neighbours were bitterly discussing the German invasion, when one of our German neighbours, an immigrant from Germany, walked in.

Someone said, "Here is one of them now. Give me a knife and let's get rid of him."

Father spoke to them in Ukrainian. "Don't be foolish. This man has had nothing to do with what is happening in Europe. Leave him alone."

They did not touch him.

I do not recall ever hearing a harsh word spoken in our home by our parents. We were very poor but a happy family. It is a common practice in families to celebrate special occasions in the life of family members, such as birthdays, anniversaries, graduations, and other notable events. We give gifts and cards, have cakes, light candles, and have special meals with family and friends. There is a tendency to determine our worth, or how much we are loved, by the value of the gifts, the expense of the card, or the splendor of the party. I do not remember, not even once, that we had a birthday or an anniversary party.

I remember years when I did not remember that it was my birthday until a few days after the date. There wasn't any money to buy gifts. And, even if there had been, there was nothing in the general store to buy. The store had groceries, axes, hammers, nails, tools, but no toys or trinkets. There was no Wal-Mart or Dollarama. There were no credit cards so we could buy now and pay an exorbitant interest fee for the privilege of paying later. It was all "cash and carry." If you did not have the cash, you could not carry.

We exchanged names at the Gamefield School to buy some small gifts at Christmas. All our names were put in a hat and we had to buy a small gift for the name we had drawn. The minimum we were asked to spend on a Christmas gift was ten cents. Some families could afford to spend more, and we always hoped, when the names were drawn, that one of the richer kids would have drawn our name.

The only other gift we ever received was a Christmas candy bag at the church children's Christmas program. Besides some candies, peanuts, and an apple, there was a box of Cracker Jack Popcorn with a small dinky toy or whistle in it. We were always so excited over that Christmas candy bag. We didn't ever have popcorn, peanuts, or apples, so it was a gift we thoroughly enjoyed. That small brown paper bag of Christmas candy, nuts, and a dinky toy gave us more pleasure than the expensive gifts wrapped in colourful gift-wrap.

There is a saying, "There is none poorer than he who has no family!" We had a family and we were indeed very rich in our poverty.

Homesteading Was a Lonely Life

Even when our father was off working somewhere else, we were a family. We had each other and a church fellowship with whom we met regularly. Others were not so fortunate. They had left their families in faraway countries to come alone to Canada in search of a better life. The worldwide depression made it impossible to find work and a place to live. With their funds depleted, they couldn't return to their families and home. Their only option was homesteading.

Bachelors managed to build a small, one-room houses with a homemade bunk bed, table, and stools. There were no books or radio for entertainment. Besides, many of them couldn't read or write. They couldn't have any livestock, cows or horses, for when they found work somewhere else there was no one there to look after the animals. It was a lonely life. Their only distraction was a deck of cards and games of solitaire. They would dig up a small plot for a garden and pick some berries in the bush to can for preserves. The water in their hand-dug wells was stale from lack of usage. Bloated dead mice that had fallen in and drowned would be brought up in the well water bucket. For the homesteaders with animals, the well water was kept fresh with usage.

One of our neighbours was one of these lonely bachelors who in a few years went insane. My father took him on the train to Edmonton to see a doctor. The doctor sent him to the mental hospital in Ponoka, where he refused to eat the food they offered him for he thought it was poisoned. He soon died of malnutrition.

Another bachelor married and they had a baby boy. The husband left her and the newly born baby in the one-room log house when he got some work elsewhere. Of course, there was no correspondence, and the young newlywed mom with the baby was convinced that her husband had deserted her. We were her nearest neighbour only a mile away. I can still remember seeing her crying, carrying her baby wrapped in a blanket as she came to our home. My mother tried to convince her that her husband would soon be coming back but she couldn't believe it. The police were alerted and they came and took her away. She ended up in the mental hospital in Fort Saskatchewan. Her husband came home to an empty house not knowing where his wife and baby were. Another neighbour was caring for the baby. His wife never returned to the homestead or her husband. The father raised the son on his own, and the child never got to know his mother. Homesteading was a hard and lonely life. When the economic depression ended, many of the bachelors left their homesteads.

Neighbours on the Homestead

Homesteaders, by and large, were quick to band together and help each other in the time of crisis. In the spring of 1936, the neighbour whose land bordered ours to the west was burning off some dead grass, which was a common practice so the new grass would be exposed for the animals to graze. He had a flock of sheep that needed grass. It was a Sunday, hot and dry, a good day for burning off old grass.

However, the grass fire got out of control and rapidly spread to the trees on our land and headed directly toward our farmyard. The neighbours quickly rallied with buckets of water and spades, and managed to save the barn and house. We children were put on a wagon and sent to a neighbour about a mile away. Thanks to the neighbours, our loss was minimal. Only the woodpile and some building logs that were ready to be squared with a broad axe to build a new barn were lost in the fire.

The community of immigrants got along very well with each other most of the time. There were no locks on the doors, and anyone could enter at any time. This was common hospitality. If you were cold, you were welcome to stop awhile and warm yourself. If you were thirsty you could stop and have a drink, even if there was no one at home. However, a few could not be trusted to be neighbourly. Things, and sometimes food supplies, would disappear. Everyone pretty well knew where it might have gone. My father on one occasion could not find his hammer, so he went to the neighbour to borrow a hammer. The husband was not home, so his wife went to the shed and gave my father a hammer. My father immediately recognized the tool as his. When he finished, he returned the hammer without saying anything, and went and bought himself another. Father said that his neighbour probably needed that hammer more than he did.

Some of the homesteaders came there to escape the long arm of the law, thinking that they would not be found in that undeveloped wooded region. Some probably got away with it, while others were discovered and taken away by the Royal Canadian Mounted Police. One such man, a brother to one of our neighbours, suddenly appeared and moved in with his brother. Some years later the police came and took him away and we never saw him again.

One of the illegal activities that many of the homesteaders were involved in was brewing moonshine. Their stills were usually well hidden away from the eyes of the law in the dense bush somewhere. We would stumble upon them in our squirrel hunting and berry picking. Moonshining was a means to make a few dollars. There were no hotels or liquor stores. The moonshiner's alcohol was all that was available. To those who felt that alcohol was an essential, the moonshiners were meeting a real need. During World War II, when everything was rationed, people would come from faraway places, in shiny new cars, to stock up, or top up, their liquor supplies for weddings and other occasions.

Whiskey was not only a source of income, but also the cause of hardships and heartaches. Drunkenness then, like today, disrupted family and community relationships. We had no community halls or committees planning social events, and no curling rinks or any other organized sports where people would congregate. In our community, quite regularly someone would open their home for a community dance. They would remove the furniture from one room and the neighbours were invited to a house dance. Someone would bring a fiddle or a small button accordion and the fun would begin. There was always lots of home brew available. The evenings usually ended in a brawl. Somebody did not like the way his neighbour danced with his wife, or some other minor irritation would surface. The evening would end with neighbours angry and not speaking to each other. However, when they sobered up, and were again on speaking terms, it was time for another home dance.

After the school was built, the dances would sometimes be held in the schoolhouse. When a neighbour had been offended by one of his neighbours, the offended neighbour took revenge by reporting the location of the offender's still to the RCMP. The offender would end up paying a hefty fine or spend a couple months in jail.

One moonshiner was well known to the police and they regularly visited to check things out at his place. One day, he was busy in the cow barn when he saw the police again drive onto his yard. He had a gallon or two of brew in a cream can, in the barn, and he knew the police would soon come to the barn to check things out. He quickly emptied the moonshine in the cream can into a bucket, and gave it to one of the cows to drink. The cow liked the brew, and the bucket was empty by the time the police came to the barn. Just as the police came into the barn, the moonshiner was releasing the drunk, staggering cow from the barn.

The police asked, "Why is that cow walking like that?"

The moonshiner replied, "She has been in the barn a long time and is happy to get out."

That drunken cow saved the moonshiner from a hefty fine or time in prison.

Another moonshiner had some brew in a cream can in the kitchen when the police arrived at his door. He quickly told his wife to sit on the cream can and not to move.

When the police came into the house, the moonshiner said, "You'll have to excuse my wife for not getting up. It's that time of the month for her."

The police searched the house for moonshine and found nothing.

Drunkenness was a problem in many homes. Those who made the stuff also drank it. It did not take much home brew to put one into a drunken stupor. I remember the occasion when one of the bachelors in the community got married and everyone was invited to his house to celebrate. The schoolteacher, along with a number of us pupils, was also there. There was lots of moonshine available and everyone that wanted drank freely. By the end of the day, our teacher had drunk somewhat too freely and was unable to walk so he started to crawl home on his hands and knees. We the school pupils were amused by the sight and followed him for a ways. I still wonder to this day if he got home that night or if he slept it off somewhere on the roadside. Often horse-drawn buggies and wagons would be headed home past our place with drivers slumped over. The horses knew where to go to get their drunken masters home.

Around 1950, someone built a hotel in Newbrook. Some of the drinking then shifted from the homestead log houses to the hotel. One really cold night in the middle of winter, we were in Newbrook in the evening. As we were walking down the street about half a block from the hotel, we saw this man lying in the snow between two buildings. We stopped to investigate, and discovered it was one of our bachelor neighbours. He was too drunk to wake up, or stand up. We did not know how he got to town, because he did not have a car or any horses. We knew that if we left him there, he would in a short time freeze to death. So we picked him up and put him in the back seat of our car, and took him home. We carried him into his house and put him in his bed and stoked the fire in the stove and left. I wonder if, when he awoke from his drunken stupor, he tried to figure out how he got home. It never ceases to amaze me how we intelligent human beings can sink so low to think drunkenness is an acceptable lifestyle. Maybe we are not as intelligent as we think.

Reminds me of a story I heard. Two people were walking along a country road when they came upon a sow wallowing in the mud by the roadside. A drunkard had stumbled and had fallen into the mud with the pig.

One of the pedestrians, seeing the drunkard lying in the mud puddle with the pig, commented, "One is known by the company one keeps."

The pig instantly arose and left the drunkard to wallow alone in the mud puddle. Drunkenness is truly a disgraceful bane in society.

We used to sing the hymn, *Where Could I Go But to the Lord*. One verse in this song says, *"Neighbours are kind, we love them every one. We get along in sweet accord."* I think we loved our neighbours. However, there were some we could not get along with in sweet accord no matter how hard we tried.

Every homesteader was required by law to build a quarter mile of fence on each border of his homestead, which was half of the border on each side. Their neighbour was required to build the other quarter of a mile. A 160-acre piece of land, called a quarter of a section, was a half-mile square parcel of land. Four quarters of land is called a section. If your quarter bordered a road allowance, then you were responsible to fence that whole half-mile.

The south side of our homestead quarter bordered a lazy, irresponsible homesteader's land. We had built our half of the fence. His half of the fence would have gone through a wooded area, so he just didn't bother to build it. Our animals did not wander into that area because there was no grass there. However, one of our horses discovered that the neighbour had a field of grain on the other side of the trees and could not resist the temptation to go feast on it. Every community had an animal pound. It was a prison for animals that had strayed away and gotten into a neighbour's grain field. The neighbour could take your animal to the pound, and the owner would have to pay a pound fee and pay for the damage. Well, our lazy neighbour caught our horse in his grain field and took her to the pound, which was two miles north of our place. We went to the pound, paid the fee and the damage that the neighbour said the horse had done. We brought the horse home and turned her out to pasture.

The very next day, our father saw the neighbour coming down the road again, leading the same horse to the pound, as it had returned to feast again in his grain field. He had to lead the horse past our place to get to the pound. It was also against the law to interfere with a neighbour taking your animals to the pound. Father went out to the road, stopped the neighbour, and asked him what he was doing.

The neighbour said, "Your horse got into my grain field again."

My father reminded the neighbour that there was no fence there to keep the horse from getting into his grain. Father told him to release the horse and build a fence to keep the horse out of his grain field. He refused to release the horse and raised his hand with a hammer in it and threatened to strike my father. Sefrin, my eldest brother, saw what was happening and snuck up behind the man and snatched the hammer from his hand. He then became frightened and released the horse. About two weeks later, my father received a notice to appear in court on an assault charge. When father arrived at the court, the neighbour had brought our other neighbour, his friend who lived across the road from us, as a witness to the assault. The judge asked the lazy neighbour where my father had hit him and if anyone had seen the bruises. He said he had shown the bruises to his wife. The judge asked him to show him the bruises and he had none to show. Then the judge questioned the other neighbour, who was supposed to have seen the assault, and soon found out he could not have and had not seen anything. The judge gave our lazy neighbour a good tongue-lashing, and told him to go home and build his portion of the fence right away, which he did. The judge reprimanded our father for stopping the neighbour on his way to the pound. The judge then dismissed the charges.

There were a number of other instances of neighbour conflict. One spring we ran out of feed for our animals. We needed a load of hay to tide us over for about a week until the new grass could be grazed. One of the farmers, two miles west, had extra hay and was willing to sell us a load for an agreed price of ten dollars. It was poor quality slough hay, but we needed something. We did not have the money right then and the farmer trusted us to pay him later. When we had the money, we met the man in the neighbourhood general store and offered to pay him. He would not accept the money. For some reason, he expected us to come to his farm to pay for the hay. We did not have the time, nor did we feel that we should have to make an extra trip. We tried one more time to settle up when he was driving past our farm. We went out to the road and offered to pay for the hay. Again he refused, saying that we should come to his place and give him the money, because that is where we got the hay. We were baffled by this kind of thinking and wondered why he would not take the money when we offered it to him. In a few weeks' time, we received a registered letter from a law firm in Edmonton demanding fifteen dollars for the load of hay. Because my parents could not read or write in English, I was asked to respond to this demand. I wrote a letter to the lawyer explaining that we had tried to pay the agreed price of ten dollars for the hay on a couple of occasions and our neighbour had refused to accept the money. I told the lawyer we were still willing to pay the ten dollars, which we had agreed to, which was more than the load of slough hay was worth, but we would not pay the requested fifteen dollars. The lawyer responded and told us to send the ten dollars, which we gladly did, deducting the cost of the money order and the two postage stamps. We learned later that the lawyer withheld five dollars for his services so our neighbour in the end received less than five dollars for his slough hay.

We later learned that the farmer had been counseled by the local storekeeper, a churlish, simple-minded man. We had previously sold the storekeeper an acre of land so he could relocate the store from the railroad to the highway. This acre was in a corner of a cultivated field. The back of the store was the storekeeper's family residence. During the busy springtime, we always got up at daybreak to work in the field. Sef got up early and plowed the land around the store with an old tractor that did not have a muffler. The storekeeper apparently did not appreciate being awakened at six or earlier by our noisy tractor.

My brother, Reinhart, was harrowing that same field later that day. Harrowing prepared the land for seeding. You hitched four horses to a beam that had four harrows attached to it. The harrows had rows of five-inch iron spikes that broke up the clods of earth in preparation for the seed to be sown. A teamster walked behind the harrows in the process. It was a very dusty and tiring job to drive the horses back and forth all day and trudge in loose earth behind the harrows. When Reinhart came to the end of the field next to the store, the storekeeper came over the fence and started to beat Reinhart up. Reinhart was eighteen years old, five-foot-ten, and probably weighed about 150 pounds. The storekeeper was six-two and weighed about 250 pounds. There was an unobstructed, clear view of the store from our farmyard. My father happened to be watching, and saw the big man pounce on Reinhart. Father dashed to Reinhart's aid. I guess when the storekeeper saw our father coming full speed, he made a quick retreat to the store. Our parents did not think that an assault of that nature should be ignored. So they reported it to the police. The police charged the storekeeper with assault. The storekeeper was found guilty, and had to pay a fine. From that time on he tried to find ways for revenge. Counseling the farmer not to accept payment for the hay was an attempt to get even with us. It didn't work.

Christian Fellowship

Our parents were staunch Baptist Christians, and didn't have much in common with the people in our immediate community who were mostly Catholic and Lutheran. There were a few other believers in the region. There was a community of the Brethren Faith in the Ellscott area that had house meetings. Then in the Newbrook area, there was a Standard Church. There were also a few Baptist families in the Ellscott region, seven miles north of our homestead. They did not have a church, but met together in house meetings. Our parents became good friends with these German Baptists and would get together at each other's homes for Bible studies, worship, prayer, and fellowship.

Newbrook and Ellscott believers meet at the Drisners

At Newbrook, eight miles south of the homestead, there was a larger group of German Pentecostal Believers with whom they also had fellowship. Rev. Julius Schatkowske, an itinerant Pentecostal Bible teacher and church planter, visited the Ellscott Baptists and they embraced the Pentecostal faith. After that the Newbrook and Ellscott Believers would occasionally meet at the Drisner homestead for joint fellowship meetings. The small group in Ellscott all moved away to the Okanagan Valley in British Columbia, so our parents connected with the German Pentecostals at Newbrook. The Newbrook church at first met in homes, but the group soon became too large for home meetings. Then they met for a while in the upstairs space above Eckert's store. It was soon decided that they needed to have a building. Ed Muth had a farm a half-mile north of the Newbrook village, and he gave the church an acre of land and the congregation got together and built a log church.

Building a log church

Going to church

Fellowship and worship were very important to our parents and they were consistent in their attendance at the Newbrook Church. It was a two-hour drive in a Democrat, one way, with a nearly two-hour worship and fellowship time. (A Democrat was a two-seated carriage drawn by two horses.) It pretty well took up the whole day every Sunday. We would do our farming chores in the morning and leave for church at eleven, arriving back home at five in time for the evening chores.

The Newbrook Church was led by lay people. I do not know if they could not afford to pay a pastor, or if there just wasn't any pastor available. The church service format was singing hymns, testimonies of what God had done or was doing in their lives, praying, and sharing fellowship. Lay members of the church took turns preaching. Many, like my father, were uneducated. They could read the Bible, as they had been taught how to read German by either their parents or in some cases by a church sponsored Saturday school. The sermons were usually very simple and boring: reading a Scripture and making some comments. So, we did not drive that far because of the preaching. They occasionally had guest itinerant preachers come to the church, which were a blessing.

Newbrook Congregation – 1935

In spite of all its shortcomings, the church still very profoundly impacted our lives. Not only did the church not have a pastor, but it did not have a piano or organ. All the singing was *a cappella*. Initially, there were no church programs for the children or youth. We went to church because it was a break from the work routine, and we were able to be with some other people besides the family. In spite of all this, a number of the youth of this log church entered the ministry as pastors and missionaries, and others were faithful deacons and workers in various churches over the years. To this very day, a number of pastors and missionaries around the world can trace their roots to the Newbrook Church.

The church eventually became an English interdenominational congregation. Others who moved into the area came to worship because it was the only church in the community. The Lutherans, who had built a nice church with a spacious residence for the pastor, had locked their doors. I do not know if it was because they could not afford to pay a pastor or if they could not get a pastor to come live in the area. The pastor of the Lutheran church served both the Newbrook and the Ellscott congregations. He had a Sunday morning service in Newbrook, then drove fifteen miles in a one-horse buggy, or sleigh in the winter, to Ellscott for the afternoon service, then the trip back to Newbrook before nightfall. This routine may not have been too taxing in fair weather in the summer, but it was another thing to endure in a rainstorm or winter blizzard. In 1950, after the Lutherans had discontinued services, the Pentecostals bought their church.

Newbrook Church – 1950

It was in this Newbrook church that I encountered God. It was a life-transforming experience that determined the future course of my life. The Bible states, *"Therefore if any a man be in Christ, he is a new creature, old things are passed away; behold, all things are become new"* (2 Corinthians 5:17, KJV). It was an undeniably real, life-changing experience. It happened at an evening service. A young lady, Ruth Muth, was the speaker at a series of evangelistic meetings in the church. As usual, we had attended every service with the family. I was in my late teens and was not particularly interested in spiritual things. The church was packed full and I was in the back row. At the end of the service, the evangelist had us all stand and gave an altar call, inviting anyone to whom the Holy Spirit was speaking to come forward for prayer. I was familiar with the routine and had no intention of responding. However, this evening, as we stood there, I burst out in uncontrollable weeping.

Harvey Johnson was standing beside me. He said to me, "If you want to go to the altar, I will go with you." Harvey was a graduate of the Church of God Bible School in Camrose. At the altar, Harvey opened his Bible to 1 John 1:9 and had me read it. *"If we confess our sins, he is faithful and just to forgive us our sins and to cleanse us from all unrighteousness"* (KJV).

Harvey asked me, "What does this verse say you have to do?"
"Confess my sin."
"What does it say God will do?"
"He is faithful and just to forgive my sins."
"What will be the result?"
"I'll be cleansed from all unrighteousness."

Then Harvey asked me to pray a prayer of confession, which I did. When I left the church that evening, everything looked brighter. I had an awareness of God's presence, and a quiet assurance that somehow everything was going to be okay.

Twelve people responded to the altar call that night, and made commitments to serve the Lord. We have all heard the expression that life begins at forty, or some other age or thing. But real life begins when we open the door of our hearts and let Jesus come in.

Growing Up on the Homestead

I was only two when we moved to the homestead. I do not remember much of my preschool years. I did not know we were poor or that we were deprived of anything in life. Everyone in our community just lived off the land and ordered what we could not buy at the small general store from the T. Eaton's catalog in Winnipeg. The fall order from the Eaton's catalog was new bib overalls for the boys, which had to last for a year, and a pair of felt boots for everyone with pullover rubbers to keep our feet from freezing over the winter months.

I remember the corral our father had to make to keep the animals from wandering off. During the day the cow was tethered where there was grass. The horses were hobbled by tying their front feet together with a rope, so they could not wander away. With their front feet tied, the horses had to hop and they were not able to wander very far. Father didn't have a posthole auger to auger holes for the posts, nor a maul with which he could drive posts into the ground. To build a rail fence for a corral for the cows and horses at night, he had to have something to attach the fence rails to. He first cut some short rails about five feet long, then took some thin willow twigs and tied two rails together in the middle to form an X which were set up for fence posts. These were placed about ten feet apart in a zigzag fashion on the perimeter of the corral. Long fence rails were then placed in the X and secured with more willow twigs. It was a lot of hard work but it had to be done.

I also remember the rails Dad had attached to the house before the henhouse was built. It was for the chickens to roost on at night so the coyote, skunks, weasels, and other predators could not get at them. I remember Mother making nests in boxes and putting eggs in them for clucking hens to hatch. Clucking hens were hens that had the urge to hatch some eggs. We did not have an incubator and could not afford to order hatched chicks from Edmonton, which we did later. So we relied on the clucking hens to hatch the eggs so we would have chickens to roast and hens to lay eggs. Mother would choose twelve eggs and put them in the nest and put a clucking hen in the nest. I think it took three weeks for the eggs to hatch. So it was a long-term commitment on the part of the clucking hen. The clucking hen could only leave the nest for short periods during the twenty-one days, for if the eggs cooled off the embryos would die, and there would be no chicks. So the clucking hens were watched very carefully. Some hens would get tired of sitting on the eggs and would desert the nest. Then mother would quickly try to find another clucking hen to sit on the eggs to complete the hatching. How would we know if a hen was a clucking hen? Hens normally are very quiet. When hens were clucking, they would spread their wings and go around noisily clucking, and were easily recognized. The amazing thing was that after the chicks were hatched, the hen would assume responsibility to care for and protect the chicks she hatched, and the chicks would recognize her as the mother hen, even though she did not lay the eggs. If a hawk happened to fly over the barnyard, the hen would cluck an alarm and all her adopted chicks would come running and disappear under the protection of the mother hen's wings.

The other amazing thing was that there were many birds flying over the barnyard: ducks, crows, and prairie chickens, to name a few. How did the mother hen recognize the hawk flying overhead and sound the alarm? Who taught them what a hawk looked like and to be aware? Instinct? There were other hens in the yard, but how did the baby chicks know which hen was their mother? We learned a lot from nature around us and from the barnyard animals.

For instance, when a cow gave birth to a calf, the first thing the calf would do was struggle to stand and then it would seek its mother's udder for nourishment. How did it know? This was true of all the barnyard animals.

We learned all about procreation from the farm animals. We knew that to have babies you had to have a male and a female mate. At first we only had one cow. When the cow desired to mate, we had to lead her sometimes miles away to find a bull. Once we had a few cows, we acquired a bull that was with the cows so the cows no longer needed our assistance. The bull knew what to do without our assistance, and met their needs when they desired him to do so.

We had to do the same with our sows. Usually we had to leave the sow with the boar, the male pig, for a day or so before the procreation process was completed. For the horses, there were owners of stallions that would go from one farm to the next.

We had to have a rooster for the hens. Good laying hens usually laid about one egg each day. To hatch chicks from these eggs, they all had to be inseminated or fertilized by a rooster. The rooster or roosters would be in the yard with the hens. When a hen wanted an egg fertilized, she would squat when the rooster came by and the rooster would inseminate the eggs that were developing in her. With dozens of hens in the barnyard, the rooster was a very busy fellow all day long.

At the time we were growing up, there was no sex education in the schools and the subject was tabooed by the public. There was no TV to view or girly magazines or books to read on the subject. But we farm children were very well informed because we saw procreation enacted on a daily basis.

We learned a lot on the farm by experience that city kids did not have the opportunity to learn. We learned how to work with animals: how to milk cows, shear sheep, harness horses, build fences, butcher pigs, and how to remove the bristles from the pig, smoke bacon, butcher and skin beef, chop a chicken's head off and pluck off the feathers, and much more.

One problem that plagued the homesteaders was the gophers. They were everywhere and stood erect like sentinels in the seas of yellow dandelions. They were there before the homesteaders arrived. It was not only that their burrows destroyed growing grain in the cultivated fields, but the multitude of squeakers also ate huge swaths around the burrows.

In the 1930s, the Social Credit Provincial Government in Alberta implemented a program to control the gopher population. To encourage the farmers to cull gophers on their land, they paid one cent for the tail of every gopher killed. Farmers could bring the tails to schoolteachers or storekeepers, who would sign declaration forms. We used a variety of methods to catch and kill the gophers so we could cash in on the penny bounty. Some made binder twine snares, which they would place over the gopher hole. Then they would lie on the ground some distance from the burrow and wait for the gopher to come out. When it did, they would yank the twine and snare the gopher. Where we lived there were sloughs of water. I remember the many buckets of water we poured down gopher holes. When the gophers came out to keep from drowning, our dog would snatch them and kill them and we would cut off the tail. You could actually buy something with a penny back then.

I don't know how effective our efforts were. We did this in the spring to prevent the birth of the next generation of squeaking sentinels, but there were still always many gophers doing their destructive work in the fields of grain. Eventually, we were able to acquire poison that we put in the gopher holes, which was far more effective.

Fieldwork involved preparing the fields for seeding, and the seed for sowing. Plowing a field with a walking plow was tiring to say the least. A team of horses pulled the plow, with the farmer walking behind the plow and keeping it upright and in the ground, while at the same time driving the horses. Once the field was plowed, it had to be harrowed before the seed could be sown. I remember my father wrapping a bed sheet around his shoulders to create a pouch in front that he filled with seed grain. Then he would march back and forth across the field scattering seed by the handful. This was called broadcasting. After that, the field had to be harrowed again to bury the seed in the ground so the seed could germinate without being eaten by birds. Before we had money for the steel harrows, which I described when I told the incident of my brother with the storekeeper, my father had to make a harrow. He made a triangular wooden frame out of three beams in which he drilled holes and drove pegs in the holes for harrow teeth.

Emil sowing seed by hand

There was hay to make. At first, we cut the hay with scythes, raked it by hand, and then piled it up with a rounded top to shed the rain. These were called haycocks to keep the hay from rotting on the ground when it rained. I remember Mother taking us with her to the hay field as she raked the hay together and then used a fork to make haycocks. The haycocks were later loaded on hayracks to make haystacks. While Mother was raking the hay and building haycocks, Father was cutting more hay with his scythe. We needed the hay to feed the animals in the winter. Later, we were able to purchase a horse-drawn hay mower and a horse-drawn hay rake, which made haymaking much easier.

Learning by Doing

We had to make lumber and build buildings. There were barns for the animals, granaries to store grain, a garage for the car and tractor, and a new five-bedroom house for the family.

The 1918 Ugly Duckling Tractor

We had to learn to make things and repair things. When we bought the old 1918 cross motor Case tractor, there was no mechanic in the community to fix it when it quit running, and we had no repair manual. We just had to figure it out. The list of what we had to learn to do to survive on the homestead was endless.

A couple of city slickers driving a 1928 Chevy were driving from Athabasca to Thorhild. On their way they stopped at Ellscott, and went into one of the stores to buy something to eat. Their 1928 six-cylinder Chevy was running just fine before they went into the store, but when they came out and started the car, the engine was misfiring and had little power. They drove the seven miles from Ellscott to our farm, and decided to stop on the roadside and see if they could figure out what the problem was. I saw them standing on the road by the car, puzzled. I was only sixteen at that time. I went out to the road and asked them what the problem was. They didn't know. I asked them if they would mind if I checked it out.

I am sure they thought, "What could this kid living in the bush here possibly know about engines?"

When they started the car, it did not take me long to realize that it was an ignition problem. I got a pair of pliers and a crescent wrench, removed the valve cover from the top of the engine so I could see which cylinder was supposed to be firing, and discovered that some prankster must have mixed up the spark plug wires when they were in the store at Ellscott. I simply changed the spark plug wires to their proper firing order and the car engine ran smoothly again. These two city slickers were amazed that I had discovered the problem and was able to fix it so quickly. They gave me a dollar and drove merrily on their way.

We had to learn many things out of necessity. Some we learned by doing, others because we just wanted to know. There were no technical schools, like Southern Alberta Institute of Technology (SAIT) in Calgary or Northern Alberta Institute of Technology (NAIT) in Edmonton, where one could go to learn carpentry, plumbing, or to be an electrician or any other trade. We just had to figure it out and do it.

Breaking new soil

My brother Sef was sent to Leduc to live with Uncle Sam, my mother's brother, because he had a blacksmith shop and he was to teach Sef how to be a blacksmith. The understanding was that Sef, who only had a Grade Six education, would attend school during the day and work in the blacksmith shop after school hours and on Saturdays. Sef was probably thirteen or fourteen. I don't know why Sef didn't go to school, but instead worked full-time in the blacksmith shop. Perhaps Sef preferred the shop to the classroom. Uncle Sam had designed and was manufacturing windmills. It apparently was a very good windmill, for many of the farmers wanted to buy one to pump water for their cattle from their hand-dug wells. (One of Uncle Sam's windmills is on display in the Western Museum in Medicine Hat, Alberta.) Sef was kept very busy building windmill towers, making windmills, and learning how to do many other things while he worked in the blacksmith shop in Leduc. Sef only stayed in Leduc about two years, but he learned a lot. He had a natural aptitude for carpentry, making and fixing things.

Sef learned from Uncle Sam, and we learned from Sef. When Uncle Sam gave up blacksmithing, we bought all the tools in the shop and set up a blacksmith shop on the farm. Uncle Sam then got into house building. He needed help, so Sef worked with Uncle Sam building houses in Edmonton. Sef, with a Grade Six education, eventually became the Maintenance Supervisor for all of Northern Alberta's government buildings.

When I went to work in Edmonton, Sef was working for a house builder, Golden Construction. Sef got me a job with him forming home footings. When I left Golden Construction, I got a job with Pool Construction. Pool Construction, a unionized firm, was building a Safeway store on the corner of 24th Street and Kingsway Avenue in Edmonton. I walked onto the construction site and asked for a job. They asked me what I knew about construction. I told them I grew up on a farm and we built all the buildings we needed.

They said, "Bring your saw, square, and hammer and if you can do the work we'll hire you as a carpenter."

The hourly pay was almost double of what I'd been paid as a non-union carpenter. I learned two key essentials to remember in construction: "Lined and Level." I always made sure that everything was straight and level. I did not have any problem, and later wrote the required exam and got my Journeyman Carpenter Certificate. After I had worked as a carpenter for a while, I was asked to be a foreman. Later, when I became a church planter, carpentry skills proved invaluable. When we were in a church that was unable to pay an adequate salary, I could always augment my pay by doing some carpentry. My carpentry was also useful in church maintenance and church construction. "Lined and Level" is also a good principle to live by. Living a straight and honest life, and always being upright in everything is a good way to avoid problems in our lives.

The new barn

Improvement on the homestead came slowly. The original log barn was replaced by a bigger barn with a hip roof. The cattle herd was increased, and a flock of sheep was added. There were more pigs in the pigsty. Pieces of farm equipment were purchased that lightened the workload. Eventually, we purchased a milking machine to milk our fifteen cows. We also bought a Johnson Iron Horse air-cooled engine to pump water from the well for the animals.

We boys moved out of the house and slept in the barn hayloft for the summer. Another chicken barn was needed and built, and we boys slept there for a while before the chickens moved in. In the mid-1940s, Sef went to Edmonton and, I believe with the help of Uncle Sam, bought a used 1940 Hudson car. We built a garage for the car, and the newly acquired Cockshot 30 tractor. Since the chickens needed to move into the new henhouse, we boys had to move out, so we built a couple of bunks in one corner of the garage where we slept for a while until we built the new five-bedroom farmhouse in 1948.

Life Was Hard on the Homestead

The provincial government in the mid-1930s employed the homesteaders to clear the bush off the road allowance and build corduroy roads in the swampy areas, in return for the taxes they owed. This eliminated the zigzag trails through the bush from one farmyard to the next, and shortened the distances considerably. It also eliminated opening and closing of gates at every farm. The gates were sometimes left open and the animals would wander off, or into grain fields which frustrated the farmers. In the road building project, the government provided the scrapers, and the farmers provided the horse and manpower. The corduroy roads over the swampy areas were built by first cutting down trees and laying them side by side across the swamp. Then dirt was scraped off the nearby banks with horse-drawn scrapers and dumped on the tree rails that had been laid across the swamp. There were two kinds of scrapers: a two-horse scraper and a larger four-horse scraper. This made a good road bed for the homesteaders to travel on across the swampy areas.

The Gamefield School was built 3.25 miles north of where we lived. Before the road allowance was cleared and the swamps bridged, we had to walk 5.5 miles to get to school. Thankfully, they cleared the road allowance shortly after they opened the school, so we didn't have to do that for very long.

Life was very hard on the homestead. There were no conveniences and no luxuries, and no doctors or drug stores where we could buy pain killer pills or antibiotics. There was no national health plan or regional health services. The nearest doctor was thirty miles away, a whole day's drive in a wagon or sleigh. There was no refrigeration so food would easily and readily spoil. We would eat spoiled leftovers and get violently ill. I remember lying in bed with a high fever seeing psychedelic colours on the ceiling, sick from food poisoning. We could not be rushed in an ambulance to the nearest emergency ward to have our stomach pumped. We just had to puke it up and wait for the fever to subside.

Once, our father had a horrific toothache. There was no Aspirin or Tylenol in the medicine cabinet—as a matter of fact, there was no medicine cabinet. The nearest dentist was a day's train ride away and the train only ran twice a week. What could be done? The neighbour had a pair of pliers. Perhaps he could pull the tooth. That is what Father did. It is a good thing the neighbour yanked out the right tooth.

Our youngest brother Ben was still an infant when he got pneumonia. Father was away in Bruderheim, working in the harvest. Mother gathered us together, and she told us Ben is dying, he can't breathe. He had turned blue from lack of oxygen. Mother said we needed to pray for God to heal him. Our prayers were intense. God was our only hope. Ben instantly started to breathe and has kept on breathing for the past seventy some years.

Yes, we learned a lot on the farm and perhaps the most important thing of all was that we learned to trust God. Our faith in God has been our source of help in every hour of need.

Growing up on the homestead, we were deprived of many things that others more privileged enjoyed. However, there were many things that we enjoyed of which the more privileged could only dream. We could have a rodeo every day of the year as we rode bucking steers and horses bareback without saddles or bridles. We had a zoo in our backyard of skunks, porcupines, deer, bears— all kinds of wildlife, big and small. People will travel many miles to visit places like Pelee Park in Ontario, or the Everglades in Florida to see wildlife in their natural habitat. We had an aviary everywhere we went. The sky was full of birds, and the bushes full of nests with eggs of all colours and sizes. In the evenings we would be entertained by the nighthawks that would dive from high altitudes with a loud "Wooo" sound. The horned owls in the forest would haunt us at night with their ghostly "Tu Whoo" hoots. Choirs of frogs in every pond would crook their off-key choruses all day long. There were colourful butterflies, bees, and bugs. Wild animals, large and small, skittered or wandered through the woods. Yes, we were severely deprived of many things, but abundantly blessed in other ways. However, after a few forest fires and the farmers clearing the land for cultivation, the animals' and birds' natural habitat was destroyed. Their numbers gradually diminished and some disappeared all together.

Bath in the cattle water tank. Only in summer!

School Days

When our parents moved to the homestead, there was no school for the children. Eventually the farmers got together and petitioned the Athabasca School Division for a school. I do not know who took the initiative to contact the school division board. Large families were the norm then, so there were a number of children of school age with no school to attend.

When the land in Canada was surveyed into quarters, sections, and townships, there were allowances made for roads and schools. East and west, there was a road allowance every mile. South and north, every two miles. Every farmer had access to a public road without having to drive over a neighbour's land. There was one quarter in every township that was called the school quarter. If you happened to have acquired a school quarter, you had to surrender some land when it was required for a school to be built there. Every township had thirty-six sections of land, so provision was made for a school to be built every six miles. I assume that the school quarter would have been in the centre of each township. Our farm was just outside the three-mile limit from the Gamefield School.

The response from the Athabasca school division was that if the farmers would build a school, the school division would provide a teacher. I do not know how, or who was responsible for giving leadership to this volunteer community effort, but they managed to get it done. There were obviously enough parents concerned that their children should get an education to make the necessary sacrifices in time and effort to build a log schoolhouse.

The school was supplied with school desks, a chair and desk for the teacher, and a large blackboard at the front of the room. There was a big oil drum that had been converted into a wood burning heater in the middle of the room. The entrance door was on the southwest corner and a row of windows on the east side. There were some hooks at the back of the room for our coats, and a shelf for our lunch pails. There was a hand-dug well and two outhouses, one for the boys and another for the girls. There was no fence around the school and no playground or sports equipment, just a school building where some trees and shrubs had been cleared away. There, of course, was a wood pile, for fuel for the oil drum heater.

The school opened to about thirty students in 1936. The first teacher was a young man named Mike Schrwansky. I was seven years of age, Reinhart eight, Sef ten, and Adeline was twelve. We trudged the 3.5 miles to school to hopefully learn the three Rs: Readin', Ritin' and 'Rithmatic.

Gamefield School – 1938 with four Drisners:
2nd from the left in the 2nd and 4th rows and 2nd and 3rd from the left in 3rd row.

We all brought our own lunches, carried to school in five-pound Rogers Syrup tin pails, or lard pails that had wire handles. Our lunch was a couple slices of bread spread with Rogers Golden Syrup. In the winter, since everything in the kitchen was stiff and frozen by morning, the Rogers syrup could not be spread on our lunch bread until it thawed. So we put the syrup can into a pot of hot water on the stove. The syrup then could not be spread because it became fluid like water. So we poured the syrup on our lunch bread and put the syrup-soaked sandwiches in the tin lunch pails. On the 3.5-mile trek to school, in the winter, our lunch was frozen and remained frozen on the cold shelf at the back of the schoolroom. At noon we gnawed on our syrup-soaked frozen sandwiches and washed them down with cold water.

The first teacher at the Gamefield School, Mike Schrwansky, faced a dilemma when the school opened: he had some thirty children from ages seven to fourteen, and only a few could speak English. Adeline had gone to school for a short time in Newbrook. She stayed with the Eckert family. They owned and ran a General Store and the Post Office. Adeline worked after school hours in the Eckert home and store for room and board. In a short time, Adeline had gone from Grade One to Grade Four, and was able to speak some English. Poor Mr. Schrwansky had to teach many of his students English before he could teach us the three Rs. After about three months, he told the students that he did not want us speaking any language on the school grounds but English.

The school was ill-equipped and short on supplies not only on the playground but also in the classroom. There is a letter on file at the Athabasca School Division written by Mr. Myers, who was the secretary for the Gamefield School, listing the supplies on hand at the school. There were a few pencils, a blackboard brush, and a few pieces of chalk. Mr. Myers requested that the school division replenish the supplies before the next term began. Every pupil had a scribbler and a pencil. The teacher wrote all the lessons on the blackboard, and we the students had to copy them into our scribblers and solve the problems. We had spelling bees, which helped us to learn how to spell words. Since there were no books in the school, the teacher read us chapters from a novel.

We didn't have any books in our homes either, so we didn't really have any opportunities to learn to read. Even if we would have had books to read at home, we probably would not have had the time to read them. I read my first novel in the Edmonton University Hospital when I was eighteen years old. I was in the hospital for a day or two after I had my tonsil surgery. Somebody gave me *Anne of Green Gables* to occupy me while I recovered. I can't remember if I was able to read the whole book before I was released from the hospital. Later, on the farm, we subscribed to the Winnipeg Free Press weekly paper so that gave us something to read.

The teachers were kept busy writing lessons on the blackboard for each class. They did not have time to supervise the playground activities at recess and the noon hour. We had to plan our own games. There was Anti High Over. We chose two teams, one for each side of the school. We would throw the ball over the roof and if the ball was caught, they would run and tag someone on the opposite side. The side that tagged the most was the winner. There was Count to 100 Red Light, which was a hide-and-seek game, and Fox and Goose circles in the snow in the winter. After a while, the school acquired a ball and bat and an area was cleared for a ball diamond so we could play softball games.

Then there was a period when we were trying to catch rabbits. We had convinced the teacher that we could catch rabbits, skin them, and sell the hides and buy sports equipment for the school. So at noon, most of the students headed for the woods around the school in search of rabbits. I don't know how we thought we could catch these rabbits, as we did not have any traps or snares. But, it was fun.

The teacher that year was a mother who had five of her children in the school with her. Her husband was working somewhere else. She was an exhausted mom trying to teach over thirty children in six grades. She was, I think, happy to get us off the schoolyard for the noon hour. The problem was we wandered so far from the school that we didn't hear the school bell ring for the afternoon classes. After a while she sent one of her children to go search for us. When we heard him coming, we hid in the bush. He returned to the school and told his mother that he couldn't find us. We eventually returned to the school, shortly before it was time to go home, and told the teacher we did not hear the school bell. We did not catch even one rabbit, so we had to abandon that fundraising scheme.

That tired mom/teacher was the teacher for only one year. At the end, we all received a passing grade on our report cards. The new teacher who came in the fall tested us, and discovered we had all failed our grades. We had trudged to school through sleet, snow, and rain, cold and hot for a whole year for nothing.

Then there was the skinny-dipping episode. As I said, the teacher was always busy at recess and noon writing our lessons on the blackboard and did not have time to supervise the playground. One summer some of the students discovered a deep pond near the school and went skinny-dipping at noon. It was not long until the whole school body, boys and girls, were all skinny-dipping at noon. Some of the girls were older and well developed, which I am sure was a pleasant sight for the older boys. Well, that did not last very long. Somehow the teacher discovered what was going on, and that pleasant noonday activity came to an abrupt end.

We hear a lot about bullying in schools these days. Well, that is not anything new. We bullied and were bullied on the school grounds and on the way to and from the school. When we complained to our parents about it they would confront the bully and the bullying would end. On the unsupervised school ground, we had lots of freedom to bully. Discipline in the school house was limited to strapping the hands, sitting in the corner facing the wall in front of the classroom, or staying after school and writing on the blackboard one hundred times that you would not do that again. In the homes, parents used "corporal punishment" to teach their children acceptable behaviour. I don't recall, except for one time, that any of us were strapped or slapped. I don't remember why my father chased me through the garden one day as I tried to escape a strapping. I apparently had done something that wasn't acceptable. As Christians, our parents did what the Bible teaches.

He who spares the rod hates his son, but he who loves him is careful to discipline him.
—Proverbs 13:24, NIV

The rod of correction imparts wisdom, but a child left to itself disgraces his mother.
—Proverbs 29:15, NIV

It is the duty of all parents to *"Train a child in the way he should go, and when he is old he will not turn from it"* (Proverbs 22:6, NIV).

We were disciplined at a very early age, that's why I don't remember. From our early childhood we knew the boundaries for good and bad behaviour. Personally, in raising our children I felt that there should be as few rules as possible, and that the rules would be non-negotiable and enforced consistently. Our parents had few rules in our home and lots of freedom for us to learn by experience that bad behaviour had consequences and good behaviour had its reward. Our parents were kind, gentle, peace-loving examples. There was very little hugging or confirmation. Our reward was in the task well done for the good of all. Our parents hadn't read any of Dr. Spock books on childrearing or seen any Dr. James Dodson films on how to have a happy family. They knew by instinct what was best for their children. We and our children and grandchildren are the beneficiaries of their loving and caring instincts and insights.

During the winter, someone who lived close to the school had to go there early in the morning to light a fire in the oil drum heater to warm up the school in time for the classes to begin. At first, there was no housing for the teacher on the school grounds, so they roomed and boarded with farmers close to the school. At the beginning of World War II, the teacher at the school was an elderly lady. Her name was Maude Moore. Just that year, the school division had provided a one-room house on the schoolyard for the teacher. Maude Moore was very patriotic. She bought war bonds and encouraged others to do the same. That winter we had an abnormal amount of snowfall. One night, the teacher's house caught on fire. Maude Moore escaped from the burning house in her nightgown and stumbled a half-mile through deep snow in the dark to the nearest farm. By the time she got to the Krause farm, the teacher's house and everything in it was a heap of smoldering ashes. For Maude Moore, the greatest loss in that fire was the war bonds she had purchased.

When we arrived at the school the next morning and saw the smoldering ashes, we didn't know if we still had a teacher, or if she was part of the smoldering ashes. Entering the school, we found her seated in the teacher's chair behind the teacher's desk dressed in some borrowed clothes from Mrs. Krause's closet. Up to that point, Maude Moore was probably the most experienced and best teacher the school had. She was small in stature and somewhat stooped. She had a problem disciplining the older boys in the school. They towered over her. Strapping their callused farm hands did not hurt them, but only exhausted the exasperated teacher. They were too big to make them sit in the corner in front of the classroom. The only other option was to have them stay after school and write on the blackboard one hundred times that they would not do this misdemeanor again. At the end of the day, we always stood and sang *God Save the King*. One day Maude Moore announced, before we sang, that one of the older boys was to stay after school was dismissed. While we were singing, the delinquent teenager dashed out the door. Maude Moore had us all sit down again, for what seemed like a long time before she gave us permission to go home. The delinquent teenager either was not allowed back to school or, with the parents' blessing, made the choice to stay home to work on the farm.

My brother Reinhart was not academically inclined and was, to the teacher's frustration, easily distracted. One day the teacher asked Reinhart to stay after school and write on the blackboard 100 times, "I will not waste time in school." Reinhart got the message. He decided if going to school was a waste of time, he would stay home and work on the farm. He was probably twelve at the time, and very able to do much-needed farm work. His decision pleased everyone. The teacher was happy, my parents were happy for the extra help, and Reinhart was happy. With only a Grade 3 education, Reinhart became an exceptionally successful farmer and eventually took over the family farm. He knew animal husbandry and was a good mechanic capable of maintaining all the farm equipment. He learned to weld and do carpentry, and built the required buildings on the farm. Yes, for Reinhart, "School would have been a waste of time."

Most of the children quit attending Gamefield School after the sixth grade. I wanted to stay in school, so I went on to eighth grade. That was as far as I could go at the Gamefield School. There was no high school, so my parents arranged for me to go live with a farm family west of Abee, about six miles north of Thorhild. There I could attend the Tudor High School. This was my first experience away from home, and there was no way to communicate with my parents. It was late fall and I needed new shoes. The soles of my old shoes were worn out with holes in them. I also needed warm winter clothes. So one day, the farmer decided to take me home to see my parents and to get some of the things I needed.

When I got home, a decision was made for me to stay at home. The Athabasca School Division had decided to open a new school, the Alpen School. It was in a rented farmhouse one mile from our home. The teacher, Bill Penchuk, was willing to teach me Grade 9. He would teach all the students from grades one to nine. I was the only Grade 9 student that school ever had. At that point, all Grade 9 students had to write the provincial examination to qualify for high school. I had to write the same exam as the city children that attended well-equipped schools with a teacher for every grade. I was not sure if I would make it. However, Mr. Penchuk did his best to prepare me for high school and to all our amazement, I made it. I did not have the opportunity to go any further academically. However, I did have the sole distinction of being the best-educated person in the community.

The farm prospered. On top of our new five-bedroom house, we acquired more land, and increased the herd of cattle and the acreage under cultivation with new farm equipment. We harvested the forest of the big trees for lumber. We were able to acquire a serviced lot in Edmonton in 1950, and built a small two-bedroom house with the lumber from the farm. Sef was working in Edmonton and he lived in the basement of the unfinished house. While he worked, he finished the upstairs in his spare time.

Aerial view of the farm.

Facing the Future

What about me? I was now an adult, twenty years of age. What was I going to do with my life? I was given life, but for what?

I had become what I was, but what was I going to do with what I was? Had I been given life to slop pigs, milk cows, make hay, clean barns, plow fields, sow and reap? Perhaps marry and have a family with a pretty neighbourhood girl with a Grade Six education.

Somebody said, "It matters not how long you live, but how." But how should one live to get the most out of the gift of life that was given to us by God? For some it would be the farm, to grow food to feed the hungry. For others, it could be a profession to bring health to the sick, help to the needy, or some other service to humanity. How was I to live? What was I to do with the life God had given me?

Because of my allergies to grain dust, farming wasn't an option. There were pretty young ladies in the community, but I had committed my life to the Lord Jesus. As a believer, I knew that a marriage partner had to be more than a nice figure, good looks, and good cooking skills.

The Bible speaks about the path of life:

Thou wilt shew me the path of life; in thy presence is fulness of joy; at thy right hand there are pleasures for evermore.
—Psalm 16:11

God has a plan and purpose for every life. However, we are born in sin, and as long as we are living in sin, we cannot know God's plan and purpose for our lives, because sin separates us from God. Christ, as our Saviour, came to remove the wall of sin that kept us from knowing God's plan and purpose for our lives.

But now in Christ Jesus ye who sometimes were far off are made nigh by the blood of Christ. For he is our peace, who hath made both one, and hath broken down the middle wall of partition between us.
—Ephesians 2:13–14

How does God reveal His plan and purpose for our lives? Does He speak in an audible voice? Send a message on Facebook? Is it by way of a prophet? A sign in the sky? A dream in the night? God may well use any of these and hundreds of other ways, but most of the time it comes without fanfare, just an open door for us to enter through.

I happened to be in Edmonton for a few days in the early fall of 1951. One Sunday evening, I attended the evening service at the 108th Street Pentecostal Church. Fulton Buntain, the son of D.N. Buntain, the pastor of the church and founder of the Canadian Northwest Bible Institute (CNBI), now Vanguard, announced that Bible school classes would begin in a few weeks. Anyone interested should go downstairs after the service to register.

The thought of going to Bible College had never entered my mind. However, I was now an adult and it was time to decide what I would do with my life. What were my options? Because of my allergy to grain dust I couldn't remain on the farm! I had accepted the Lord as my Saviour and committed my life to God. I was aware that the Scriptures declare that the steps of a righteous man are ordered of the Lord.

For me, the future seemed like a blank page full of uncertainties. I can't say that I prayed about going downstairs after the service to register to be a student at CNBI. There was no voice from heaven thundering, "This is what God wants you to do!" I didn't consult my parents, or anyone else. I just went downstairs and signed up.

Growing up on the farm and being a farmer, I developed a pragmatic approach to life. One just has to do what needs to be done when the occasion arises. This was one of those occasions that required a response on my part. So I did it.

When I arrived home and told my parents that I had registered to go to Bible College, they didn't disapprove of my decision. I would be missed on the farm, as there was always more work that needed doing than we had time to do. Apart from that, though, I think they were happy. I would be living with Sef in the unfinished house in Edmonton while I attended Bible College. The cost of my decision would be minimal, apart from the cost of registration, which wasn't very much back then.

I didn't know how this decision would affect my future. I certainly wanted to do the will of God, but I didn't know what that would be. I was very much aware of my inadequacies. I was still a barefooted boy from a homestead in the bush of Northern Alberta. We had been taught very little of the Bible growing up. There had been no Sunday school, or any midweek Bible studies. Church was a time of singing hymns, hearing testimonies, prayer, and listening to somebody reading a Bible text and make a few comments. Since we didn't have a pastor in the church, I knew nothing about what it meant to be a minister. My lack of knowledge of the Scriptures really made it impossible to know what I was signing up for.

My pragmatic upbringing led me to the basement church office that Sunday. The prophetic utterance of the Moravian pastor at the time of my birth had been inspired of God, and was beginning to come to fruition.

Ready to face the future

One night when I was ten years of age, I had a dream that I was traveling somewhere by train. I remember awakening, knowing I would be a minister of the gospel. It was so real and yet seemed so impossible. I did not know what that meant, and so I went on with my life on the homestead. Ten years later, I was in the basement church office signing up for Bible School, still not knowing why and where that would take me, or even realizing it was God's plan for my life.

The Bible School classes were in the church basement and began with a daily devotional at 8:00 a.m. The classes were from 8:30 a.m. to noon. Most of the students had afternoon jobs to pay their way. I worked at a gas station for sixty-five cents an hour, pumping gas and fixing flat tires. The service station was only a couple of blocks from the church. Later, I got a job at Muttart Lumber Yard for a dollar an hour. The lumberyard was some distance from the church, so I had to take a bus to work. Rony's Cafe was close to the church, so as soon as the classes were dismissed I would hurry over to Rony's to have an 85-cent full-course dinner, then catch the bus to work at the lumberyard from 1:00 to 5:00 p.m.

There was not much time at the end of the day for studying. We had to pay close attention to the lessons if we were going to learn anything. I had a Grade 9 education, some only had elementary school, and others were high school graduates. The school did not have any academic requirement for eligibility. The only requirement was that you were born again and wanted to prepare yourself to serve the Lord in some form of ministry. Like Nicodemus, I had a very limited knowledge of the Bible and spiritual things, and everything else (John 3:1–21). The lack of books at home, and in the Gamefield School, had left me with a limited ability to read. I was a slow reader with a very limited vocabulary, so it was extremely difficult to keep up or even to try to understand what we were being taught. Of course, no one got a failing grade. We all received marks for effort.

When I was still quite young, someone told me this:

Only one life to live, 'twill soon be past,
Only what is done for Christ will last.

I never forgot this. I did not know, as none of us do, what life had in store for me. Having God-loving, praying parents, we understood that God had a plan for every life. Happiness and joy in life could only be realized in knowing and doing the will of God and walking in it. But how does one find and know the will of God? The Psalmist knew the key to knowing God's will and living a full and meaningful life.

I have set the Lord always before me: because he is at my right hand, I shall not be moved. Therefore my heart is glad, and my glory rejoiceth: my flesh also shall rest in hope.

Thou wilt shew me the path of life: in thy presence is fulness of joy; at thy right hand there are pleasures for evermore.
—Psalm 16:8–9, 11

It all begins with choosing to enter into a relationship with God, giving God His rightful place in our lives. Then God can direct us in the path we should go. In that path, there is fullness of joy and pleasures for evermore. In my now sixty-some years of involvement in ministry, we came to many junctions when we did not know which way to go, or were tempted to take the wrong path. The Lord was there to show us and keep us on the right path.

That does not mean we didn't face any challenges, or that the way was always easy. There were times when we had to go through deep waters, but we found that the Lord was there with us as He promised:

When you pass through the waters, I will be with you; and when you pass through the rivers, they shall not sweep over you; when you walk through the fire you will not be burned; the flame shall not set you ablaze.
—Isaiah 43:2, NIV

Of course, not everyone is called to the ministry. But all must choose to walk with God to have the blessing of God on every aspect of their lives.

For me, the call of God to the ministry came at times when I was broken at the altar of God. One of those times was when Evangelist Fern Huffstutler spoke to the student body in my second year at Bible School. Her text was the story of Jesus feeding the multitude with five loaves and two fishes. First, before the loaves could meet the needs of the multitude, they had to be given to Jesus. Second, Jesus blessed them. Third, Jesus broke the loaves. Lastly, they had to be given to the multitude. She told us that we were the loaves. Before God can use us to meet the needs of the multitudes that are still in sin and dying, we must give ourselves to God and be anointed, blessed, and broken. She invited us to give ourselves to God. We must be willing to go to where the multitudes are dying. An unbroken loaf may be beautiful and have all the ingredients to nurture the hungry, but until it is broken it is only a decoration. Our Bible School training was necessary, but would be of little or no value without the anointing of God. We may be a beautiful loaf, gifted, and highly trained, and have a well-planned program, but if we have not been broken and blessed we will only be a loaf to be admired. That message powerfully affected me. I knelt in the church pew, weeping and being broken by God long after the other students had left the building.

God was calling me, preparing me for ministry. I knew now why I was here. I prayed, "Lord if you can use me I'll go where you want me to go. I'll be want you want me to be. I'll do what you want me to do."

That day, like the Psalmist, *"I set the Lord always before me. Because He is at my right hand, I will not be shaken"* (Psalm 16:8, NIV).

The Reg Knight family

Years later, as I was working full-time in construction and building a church in the evenings and weekends, somebody asked me what I did on the weekends. I told him I was building a church in the community of Ogden, in Calgary. He asked me how much I was being paid to do that. I told him I was not being paid.

He said, "I wouldn't do that for anybody."

I told him, "I wasn't doing it for anybody; I was doing it for the Lord, and it was a pleasure, not a task."

Love and Marriage

Bible schools are sometimes appropriately referred to as bridal schools. Shortly after I committed myself to serving the Lord, I started courting Shirley Ann Knight. Shirley was a recent nursing graduate of the Calgary General Hospital. She felt God's call upon her life, and was thinking she could go to a foreign country and work at a nursing station. The Calgary General Hospital had offered

Shirley an opportunity for more advanced training in nursing, along with a promotion to a better position. The day she was to sign up for the advanced training, she received a letter from CNBI (Canadian Northwest Bible Institute) inviting her to consider going to Bible School in Edmonton. She knew that this was of God, and that was what she should do.

Shirley Knight – 1952

Courtships usually begin with a date to a restaurant or some other special event. Our courtship began on a piano bench at the church. I was singing in a Bible school male quartet. Our class name was The Life Savers, so we were called the Life Savers Male Quartet. Shirley was able to play the piano, and we enlisted her to accompany us. We practiced at the church. After we were finished practicing and the others had left, I would move to the piano bench under the pretense that I needed help with my part. From the piano bench, the romance progressed to a Sunday lunch at the Waffle Restaurant. Neither one of us had much money, but the waffle shop was low-budget fare.

The Life Saver Quartet

New five-bedroom house, built in 1948

By the end of the school year, this romance thing had become a pretty serious matter. Shirley came out to the farm to meet my parents and the rest of the family still living there. She saw the two-room log house, the new five-bedroom home, and the farming environment where I grew up, which made me what I am. The entire family fell in love with the lovely, sweet Shirley whom I loved. I remember introducing Shirley as my girlfriend to Aunt Laura, who had just come to Canada from a Displaced Persons Camp in Germany after World War II. Aunt Laura couldn't speak any English. She carefully sized up Shirley and then said to me in German, "Marry her."

I asked her, "Aunt Laura, why should I marry her?"

"Sie hat garde beine!" (She has straight legs.)

Well I had not really noticed that, as I was too enthralled with Shirley's beautiful face, intelligent mind, and quick keen wit to notice the straight legs. Besides that, ladies weren't wearing mini-skirts back then so there wasn't much leg to be seen.

Waiting for the bus to return to Edmonton

Shirley went back to Calgary to work in the General Hospital for the summer, and I stayed in Edmonton to work in construction. Since email and texting had not been invented yet, and long-distance phone calls were expensive, we had to do our courting by letter over the summer months. I did not know much about courtship, but Shirley was very gracious and accepted my blundering attempts. I made a trip to Calgary that summer, and I cannot recall if I took the Greyhound bus or the train. The evening before I returned to Edmonton, I borrowed Shirley's father's Austin car to drive Shirley to the hospital for her nightshift. Before she went on duty, I unceremoniously and awkwardly proposed to her and gave her an engagement ring in the cramped front seat of the Austin in the General Hospital parking lot.

Shirley claims that the proposal and the ring on her finger made it difficult for her to concentrate on her duties as a nurse that night. Fortunately, none of her patients died of an overdose of drugs or neglect of duty. I returned to Edmonton and made arrangements to purchase the wedding band to match the engagement ring. I did not have the money to pay for it. The jeweler felt sorry for this lovesick pauper, I guess, and was willing to let me have the ring on a payment plan.

The Austin Car

Shirley came back to Edmonton that fall for her second year at Bible School. She went back to the part-time nursing job she had at the University Hospital and helped pay for the ring. I continued to work at Muttart Lumber during my third year at CNBI and graduated in the spring. Shirley planned the wedding and I showed up for the event, which took place in the old Eighth Avenue Pentecostal Church in Calgary on June 26, 1954, with Rev. John Watts officiating.

The Wedding Party

June 26, 1954

We had planned to spend the first night of our honeymoon in a nice motel in Claresholm. However, a dense fog had moved in, and it was not safe to travel that night. So we drove as far as Okotoks, and spent the night in a dingy old hotel. We were probably the first and last honeymooners to spend their first night in that hotel. The washroom was at the end of a long hallway, with no water or sink in the room, just a double bed. They probably changed the bed sheets once a week. The only good thing about that hotel was the price.

CNBI graduation – 1955

With my parents' help, I had acquired a used 1951 Plymouth Sedan. During my lifetime, prior to our marriage, I had not traveled very far. I had not gone beyond the borders of the province of Alberta, or stayed in a hotel or motel overnight. So, on this honeymoon trip I was suddenly overwhelmed with so many new experiences. I, the barefooted, uneducated bushman, was with a beautiful, intelligent, educated young lady. We were surrounded by the beautiful Rocky Mountains, pristine lakes, and rushing mountain streams of Waterton National Park, Glacier National Park, Okanogan Valley, and Banff. I saw things and beautiful scenery I had not known existed. Yes, it pays to serve Jesus. I had chosen to walk the path that God had for my life. And my life was full of joy and unending pleasures.

The 1951 Plymouth

When we returned from our honeymoon, we settled into a one-room apartment in Edmonton. It was close to the church and Bible School so Shirley could complete her final year of studies. Because work was scarce, I was only employed some of the time that winter. So we lived frugally on Shirley's part-time salary at the University Hospital, and my unemployment cheques of fifteen dollars every two weeks. Shirley graduated in the spring of 1955, and we entered the ministry shortly after.

The Bible School teachers did their very best to prepare us for ministry. However, I was very ill prepared for challenges we would soon face. I learned that the ministry was not for the fainthearted, feebleminded, or slackers. I also realized that I didn't have in me what it takes to do the work of the ministry. The apostle Paul said, *"I thank Jesus Christ our Lord, who hath enabled me, for he counted me faithful, putting me in the ministry"* (1 Timothy 1:12) God had called us and put us in the ministry. And, like Paul, God would enable us to do the work of the ministry.

The Ministry

The ministry is not a career choice, but a calling.

> *For ye see your calling, brethren, how that not many wise men after the flesh, not many mighty, not many noble, are called:*
> *But God hath chosen the foolish things of the world to confound the wise; and God hath chosen the weak things of the world to confound the things which are mighty.*
> —1 Corinthians 1:26–27

I certainly realized my lack of wisdom. A homesteader's son, I certainly was not noble, yet God had called me and I depended on God to enable me in my weakness to do the work of the ministry.

Like the Apostle Paul said, *"I was with you in weakness, and in fear and in much trembling"* (1 Corinthians 2:3).

Right from the very beginning, I have done a lot of trembling realizing that if I was going to be able to do the work of the ministry it would have to be in the wisdom and power of the Holy Spirit. I was always amazed at how God used what I knew as weak and feeble to touch the hearts of the people.

We entered the ministry in 1955. At that point in the history of the Pentecostal Assemblies of Canada (P.A.O.C.), there were no funds for church planting or even for a pastor's salary. If you were called to the ministry, you had to go out and start a church on your own. This meant getting a job to support your family and to finance the church planting project. My work experience on the farm qualified me as a carpenter, a mechanic, truck and bus driver, and farm worker. I did most of these things to support ourselves and finance our ministry. When necessary, Shirley often worked as a nurse.

One Saturday, Rev. Tilton, the Alberta P.A.O.C. District Superintendent, took another student and me for a drive down Highway 14 east of Edmonton. He showed us the towns along the way, such as Vegreville, Vermillion, and others, and told us that all these towns needed churches.

"You can come here, get a job, rent a hall or some other facility, and start a church."

We did not go to any of these places, for Pastor Jimmy Robertson, the pastor of the country church at Bowville, 12 miles east of Carmangay, was retiring and the church needed a pastor and we were asked to go there. Jimmy was a Scotsman and he told us the secret to surviving in the ministry.

In his Scottish brogue he told us, "To make ends meet in the ministry, you have to buy tongue and tail. There's a lot of good eatin' in the tongue and the tail makes good soup and they don't cost much."

We've been tongue-and-tailing it for the past sixty years.

What we learned on the homestead helped us survive in the ministry. If you did not have the money, you did not buy it. Common sense sometimes meant doing without some things for a while. We never seemed to lack what we really needed. God always provided, as He promised: *"But my God shall supply all your need according to his riches in glory by Christ Jesus"* (Philippians 4:19).

Over the past sixty years, we have owned and driven over thirty different vehicles. Much of the time, we needed two vehicles, because Shirley was working. We never bought a new car, but we always had reliable transportation. We learned how to maintain and repair things on the farm, and it stood us in good stead over the years.

When I retired at sixty-five, people gave us cars that were in their driveway or backyard. These cars were not running anymore and would cost too much to have a mechanic fix them. Some of them had very little wrong with them. I would repair them, sell them, or give them away. I calculate that I saved thousands of dollars over the years. Those saved dollars put shoes on our feet, clothes on our back, and bread on the table. To be a church planter, one may have to do without some things. The Apostle Paul said, *"I have learned, in whatever state I am, therewith to be content"* (Philippians 4:11).

Which is better: to have things and be discontented, or to do without in contentment?

Many of the pastors during this era were tent makers and pioneered churches that are strong and vibrant today. My carpentry was useful not only in earning a few bucks when the cupboard was bare, but it was also in building and upgrading churches. Where there was no housing provided by the church, we would buy a house to upgrade and sell for a profit when we went elsewhere. Or I would build a house for the church or our family. This way we were able to keep abreast of inflation and had a debt-free place to live when we retired.

Carmangay, Alberta: 1955

In the first week in May, 1955, my brother Reinhart brought a half-ton farm truck to Edmonton. We loaded our few belongings on the truck and headed to the Bowville Full Gospel Church, twelve miles east of Carmangay. We did not preach for a call, so we did not really know where we were headed, or what we were getting ourselves into. The church had been a dance hall at one time, before the Pentecostals bought it, probably in the late 1920s. It was an old building out on the bald prairie. The back part of the hall had been converted into the pastor's residence. There was a living room and kitchen on the ground floor, and a bedroom upstairs. The pastor's residence was furnished with throwaway furniture. There was a wood burning stove, and a wind-powered generator to keep the batteries charged up for the electric lights. A cistern under the kitchen caught and stored the rainwater off the church roof. There was a hand pump in the kitchen. This water was not fit for human consumption, but we could use it to mop the floor, and when boiled, to do the dishes. We had to drive half a mile down the road to a farmer's well for drinking water.

Bowville Church

Our first Sunday there, a dozen people attended the service. The second Sunday, Shirley and I sang hymns and prayed while we waited patiently for someone to come, but no one came. I would like to think it probably was the unusual May snowfall that kept them away, not my preaching. After that Sunday, there were only four members from the Greene family, a widower, and a farmer's wife with her two children that came to the church regularly. The offerings were small, and the pastor's salary was smaller still. However, in July we did have a good Daily Vacation Bible School (DVBS), with a number of children from nearby farms. The widower did not have any transportation, so I would drive out to his farm and bring him to church. Neighbours took him to town with them when they went to buy groceries. He always bought the same things. One was ten pounds of sugar. His house was a dusty hovel. He was too old to fix or clean up things. Whenever we visited, he would open the kitchen cupboard, get out a bag of sugar, dust it off, and give it to us.

About two months after we moved to Bowville, the Greenes informed us that they were leaving the farm and moving to Lethbridge. We informed Rev. Tilton, the District Superintendant, and we were told the church would be closed and that we should consider moving to Coaldale. So our introduction to the ministry appeared to be a total failure with the closing of the church.

The beginning of the end. Bowville Church had to be closed for lack of interest.

Glad Tidings Tabernacle – Coaldale, Alberta: (1955-1958)

The church planters of the Coaldale church were Rev. and Mrs. John Erhart. I don't know when the church started, or how long the Erharts were in Coaldale. I think John Erhart was a carpenter of sorts, for he had built a couple of houses and the church. The Erharts had considerable success, for there was at one point a sizable group of believers that worshiped in Glad Tidings Tabernacle. In the mid-1940s, there had been a hunger in the hearts of the believers for God to move in their lives. An outpouring of the Holy Spirit swept across Western Canada at that time, called the Latter Rain. This appeared to be exactly what the believers were praying for. Pastor Erhart encouraged his congregation to participate and embrace this revival of the Holy Spirit. However, it was not very long before Pastor Erhart realized that some of the doctrines the leaders of this Latter Rain revival were teaching did not line up with the Word of God. So Pastor Erhart withdrew from the revival, and began to warn the people that what was being taught was not Scriptural. He warned the people that they would put their souls in jeopardy if they continued with the Latter Rain revival. Like the church at Galatia, they were being taught another gospel, a perverted gospel not of God but of a few accursed men.

> *I marvel that ye are so soon removed from him that called you into the grace of Christ unto another gospel:*
>
> *Which is not another; but there be some that trouble you, and would pervert the gospel of Christ.*
>
> *But though we, or an angel from heaven, preach any other gospel unto you than that which we have preached unto you, let him be accursed.*
>
> *As we said before, so say I now again, if any man preach any other gospel unto you than that ye have received, let him be accursed.*
>
> —Galatians 1:6–9

Coaldale Church, 1955

The church in Coaldale did not heed Pastor Erhart's warning, and insisted on staying with the Latter Rain's so-called revival. This movement had all kinds of weird and wonderful new doctrines. One of the new revelations was that there was no longer any need for a pastor in the church to minister to the congregation. Everyone was to come to the church prepared to minister:

> *When you come together, each of you has a hymn, or a word of instruction, a revelation, a tongue or an interpretation. Everything must be done so that the church may be built up.*
> —1 Corinthians 14:26, NIV

When Pastor Erhart was told he was no longer needed, he moved to Langley, British Columbia. I believe he pioneered the Langley Pentecostal Church. Left without a pastor, the Coaldale church soon began to disintegrate for lack of leadership and financial support. The few people left did not know what to do. They did not want the responsibility of looking after the building, and there was no one left to give spiritual leadership. Some thought they should sell the building and divide the money amongst themselves. They tried, but could not find a suitable buyer. What could they possibly do?

Someone suggested that perhaps the church should be given back to the Pentecostal Assemblies of Canada. So, that is what they did. Now Rev. Tilton had the task of trying to find someone to go to Coaldale to be the pastor of this fragmented, doctrinally deluded group.

Well, there was this young upstart Reubin, and his wife Shirley, that needed somewhere to go when the Bowville church closed.

I remember driving to Coaldale and meeting with about half a dozen depressed congregants of this fragmented Latter Rain group. They were willing to have me come and be their pastor. When I posed the matter of the pastor's salary, they obviously hadn't thought of that. The common thinking in those days was that the pastor lived by faith, which most church planters had to do. However, this is not what the Bible teaches. The Apostle Paul deals very clearly on the matter of remuneration of pastors and others involved in spiritual ministries: *"Even so hath the Lord ordained that they which preach the gospel should live of the gospel[?]"* (1 Corinthians 9:14)

They told me there was no money in the treasury to pay us a salary. When I asked them about taking offerings for missions they said, "If we do that, there wouldn't be any money to pay the utilities." They did not take offerings because Jesus said, *"When thou doest alms, let not thy left hand know what thy right hand doeth"* (Mathew 6:3)

We know that Jesus was speaking of giving food and clothing to those who are in need. That's what alms are. We are not to tell anyone what we did, so we would not embarrass the recipients. Jesus was not speaking of tithes and offerings, but alms.

In the Coaldale church, there was a small locked box by the sanctuary entrance where the members were to drop their secret offerings. I was informed that I would be given the key to this secret box, and I could take all the money out and keep whatever was left over after the church bills were paid. So that was what we did. The first three months we were there, our salary from the secret box averaged out at eight dollars a month. Now if we had put more money in, we certainly would have gotten more money out. Even after the attendance had increased, the box income did not change much. The people either did not know the box was there, or they deliberately ignored it.

The church had not been completed when Pastor Erhart left. We lived in one of Pastor Erhart's vacant houses for a few months, while we constructed living facilities in the basement of the church for the pastor. We also began finishing the building. The District generously sent a monthly 25-dollar check for our support. I did some carpentry work, and was asked to drive the workers' bus that transported the people who lived in Coaldale to work in Lethbridge in the morning and pick them up to return them to Coaldale in the evening. This was also a school bus. I drove the school bus route after the trip to Lethbridge in the morning, and before the evening pickup of the workers.

We were kept very busy in Coaldale. We had two services on Sunday in the church, a midweek Bible study, youth service on Friday, and a community "Children for Christ Club." We also had Crusaders Club for boys and Missionettes Club for girls. We asked the high school principal if we could start an Interschool Christian Fellowship (ISCF) club in the school. We got permission, so we also gave leadership to that.

In Coaldale, my biggest challenge was dealing with the perverted teaching of the Latter Rain Revival many of the people had embraced. I was so new to the ministry and really knew so little that I did not know what to say or preach to counteract this warped gospel. They had been told that the church had entered a new dispensation, quoting, *"Therefore leaving the principles of the doctrine of Christ, let us go on unto perfection"* (Hebrews 6:1)

Their main doctrine was the restoration of all things. In the end, everyone will be saved, even the devil. One of the spiritual giants of the Coaldale Latter Rain believers stood up in church one Sunday morning and gave this glowing testimony that at one time he believed Heaven was a far off place, but now he knew that Heaven was here on earth, and that we can enter into a state of perfection. "Everything is going to be restored. Everybody will be saved, and I'll be walking the streets of gold hand in hand with the devil."

Since everyone will be saved, it was now no longer necessary to preach the gospel. When I preached a sermon, "The Gospel is the Power of God unto Salvation" on a Sunday evening, this man and his friend came back to the church after everyone had left to try to straighten me out in my limited understanding of the Scriptures.

I sat in our small basement kitchen with these two men as they quoted remote Scriptures from the Old Testament, proving beyond doubt that the gospel was no longer the power of God unto salvation. They said it was old doctrine that we needed to leave and go on to perfection, as obviously they had done. After a few hours, I told them that I did not know what they were talking about. I told them God had called me to preach the gospel, and until the Lord told me otherwise, I would continue to do what God had called me to do. They went away disappointed, and in a few days sent another lady over to inform me that if I did not listen to these two men and do what they wanted, I was going to lose most of the congregation. She also said we would be starved out of the church.

She, of course, had no way of knowing, and neither did anyone else, how much we were receiving from the secret box at the entrance of the church. I was certain that our income from the box was not going to change much with their leaving. The church had experienced considerable growth in a short period, and the attendance had grown from a dozen to fifty. I told their ambassador that they were all welcome to worship in Glad Tidings Tabernacle, but I could not and would not preach another gospel than what God had called me to preach.

The following Sunday we only had a few worshipers in attendance. However, most of those eventually came back, except the staunch leaders of Latter Rain. I spent most of an afternoon listening to another Latter Rain man, who had a printing shop. He had left the principles and doctrine of Christ, and gone on to perfection. He was too perfect to come to church and worship with the ordinary Bible-believing saints. This man was absolutely bald, with not a single hair on his head. He had a hearing aid in his ear that squealed occasionally, pop bottle eyeglasses, and loose clicking false teeth that he had to keep pushing back into place. He spoke with great fervor of his state of perfection. He would never be sick again and he would not die. I looked at this man with his bald head, squealing hearing aid, pop bottle glasses and his clicking false teeth, and decided that I did not want to aspire to that state of perfection.

I could not discover, in my discussions with these super saints, how one could attain this state of perfection apart from leaving the sound doctrine of Christ and embracing a perverted gospel. As the Apostle Paul, I too, over the course of our sixty years of ministry, have marveled at how people are so easily and soon removed from established sensible God-ordained ministries to that which is wacky and weird.

To mention a few: Jim Jones in the 60s, Christian Communes in the 70s, Just Praise the Lord, Jump in the River, and Five-Fold Ministry. Most, if not all of these, seem to have done little but disrupt and distract from the true purpose of the church, to declare the Gospel of the Grace of God in Christ. The perfected Latter Rain saints all died, and the river that flowed so strong for a few years seems to have gone dry; the communes cease to exist, and Jim Jones and his entire following committed suicide.

There was a song that we used to sing called *I'll Stick to the Old Fashioned Way!* It's dangerous to leave the tried and proven principles and doctrines of Christ for another gospel. We learned early in our ministry in Coaldale that it was better to stick with the tried and proven. The prophet Jeremiah talks about the people leaving the ancient, familiar, proven pathway for some new way on which they stumbled and fell.

We learned a lot about ministry in those three years in Coaldale. Our busy schedule taught us how to budget our time. We learned to trust God for our daily needs.

There were times when the cupboards were bare and there was no money for food, clothing, or gas for the car. We prayed, and God miraculously supplied all our needs. I remember at different times going to our mailbox at the post office and finding an envelope with no return address containing the exact amount of money we needed.

We did not lock our cars in those days. One morning I went out to the car and there was an envelope on the front seat with money in it. Sometimes envelopes with money were slipped under the door. Shirley was doing the laundry one day. She took the basket with damp clothes outside, and was hanging things on the clothesline. People did not have dryers back then. Some people came by and Shirley took them inside for a visit and a cup of coffee. When they left, Shirley went back to her laundry basket, and under the first item she picked up was a five-dollar bill. It had not gone through the laundry, and neither had the visitors placed it there, for they had not gone anywhere near the clothesline.

God also provided things we needed, such as a brand new fridge for our basement apartment and clothing and other items for us and our babies. John and Sandra were both born while we lived in Coaldale; John in Calgary on November 11, 1955, and Sandra at the Coaldale hospital on April 2, 1957.

I learned to wait upon God to help me preach. There were times I struggled and could not get a sermon ready. In my bare, bookless study, sitting at my homemade desk with my Bible, I cried out to God to help me. God would give me a sermon that I would readily prepare. My oration skills were limited, and sometimes I felt I had totally failed. It was at these times that someone would come to me and say, "That was just what I needed. How did you know? Thank you for that sermon."

I didn't know. Sometimes God would give me a sermon topic I did not want to preach and tried to avoid. After struggling to prepare something else I thought would be a good sermon, I would eventually give in and preach what the Lord wanted, and it was what was needed. Yes, we learned a lot about ministry in Coaldale. Things that stood us in good stead throughout the rest of our years of ministry.

We were blessed with some wonderful people in the church and friends in the community. They were ordinary, hard-working, down-to-earth people who accepted us, encouraged us, and helped us in the work of the ministry. One man came to me and said, "I can't read or write. I would like to help but I don't think there is anything I can do."

He had a very friendly, outgoing personality with a broad smile. I told him the church needed someone to greet people when they arrived. We did not have any book racks in the pews, and he could greet the people and give them a hymn book. What a tremendous blessing this uneducated, illiterate man was as he faithfully greeted everyone with a smile as they entered the church.

Another man who worked in an underground coalmine had difficulty staying awake in the service. He would fall asleep as the congregation stood to sing a hymn. When everyone sat down he would remain standing, and his wife would wake him up and make him sit down. He said to me, "I don't think I should come to church. I just can't stay awake in a warm building after working in the dark cool underground all week."

I encouraged him for his family's sake, and others, to come even if he could not stay awake for the entire service, as it says in Hebrews 10:24–25,

> *Let us consider how we may spur one another on toward love and good works. Let us not give up meeting together, as some are in the habit of doing, but let us encourage one another and so much more as we see the Day approaching.* (NIV)

Some of us may feel we do not have much to contribute so we will not be missed at church. That is not true! Just being there will spur others to be there too.

After three years of intense ministry and learning in Coaldale, the Lord opened the door for us to go to Metiskow to pastor the Full Gospel Church there. The Coaldale church was again stable and back on track with a good nucleus of people. The building was finished inside and out with a new coat of paint. I felt we had done what God had brought us to Coaldale to do and it was time for a change.

About that time, we received a written invitation to consider going to pastor the Turner Valley church. We discussed this and felt it was something we should consider, since we were already thinking of a change. We wrote a response and told the church we were interested, and would wait for a response from the church. We did not hear from them again and wondered why. A while later we received a call to go to Metiskow, which we accepted. When we packed to move to Metiskow, we discovered the letter we had written to Turner Valley church on the floor behind the fridge. We later heard that the Turner Valley Church had wondered why we did not answer their letter.

Glad Tidings Tabernacle—finished 1958

Full Gospel Church - Metiskow, Alberta

After three years of the grueling ministry in Coaldale, we needed a break or we would suffer total fatigue. When the call came in the fall of 1958 from Metiskow Full Gospel Church, we were ready to accept it. The church had a pastor's residence of a sort: two granaries put together. At least we were out of the basement and above ground, and not living in the church building. We were also receiving a salary and could budget accordingly.

Metiskow Full Gospel Church

The church was well-organized, with good leadership in every department. There was a good-size Sunday school and youth group, and an active Women's Missionary Group. There was only one weekly service, on Sunday morning. I had all week to prepare the one sermon and had time to visit the parishioners. The church had initially been founded as Pentecostal. However, people from a number of different denominations came to worship there. The church was packed full every Sunday. There were more people in church on Sunday than the population of the town, because people drove as far as fifty miles to come to church in Metiskow.

Metiskow Parsonage

The only other church in Metiskow was Lutheran. We became good friends with the pastor and his wife. Our children were much the same age, so we would babysit for each other. The two churches had never gotten along and never done anything together prior to our coming to Metiskow. Well, that changed when we were there. We jointly sponsored Christian film showings in the community hall, and other joint services such as memorial services. The Lutheran pastor and his wife were quite musical, so we formed a mixed quartet and sang at these events.

Metiskow Sunday morning worship

The salary was small, so I drove a school bus part-time. The town of Provost, thirty kilometers east, was building a new high school. I worked there as a carpenter for a while. The Pentecostals were starting a church in Provost but had no building, so I was able to help them with that project, too.

Provost Church

Glenda, our second daughter, was born in Provost on November 11, 1959, on her brother's fourth birthday. The night of her birth I went to the hospital to be with Shirley. I had worked all day and the birth of our third child was not progressing very quickly. I decided to lie down for a couple minutes on a wooden bench I found in hospital entrance and fell fast asleep. Glenda came. The nurses searched the hospital to inform me but could not find me. Someone did eventually discover me sound asleep on the bench. I sometimes wonder how many other important events I missed in life because I was not alert to what was happening.

We learn most of life's important lessons by blunders. I made my share of them. I remember one blunder I made in Metiskow that I deeply regretted. The church was founded by the Pentecostals, who believed in water baptism by immersion. Biblically, water baptism is the individual's declaration of their acceptance of Christ as their Saviour. It is symbolic and a public declaration of their transformation from spiritual death to spiritual life in Christ. However, it is not a means of grace. We are not saved because we are baptized; we are baptized because we are saved. *"He that believeth and is baptized shall be saved; but he that believeth not shall be damned"* (Mark 16:16).

The apostle Paul also states,

Know ye not, that so many of us as were baptized into Jesus Christ were baptized into his death?

Therefore we are buried with him by baptism into death: that like as Christ was raised up from the dead by the glory of the Father, even so we also should walk in newness of life.
—Romans 6:3–4

Water baptism is a declaration to the church and the world that we are going *"to walk in newness of life."*

We were going to baptize some of the believers in a nearby lake, and I wanted the candidates to know, and the church to understand, what and why we were doing this. I waxed eloquent that water baptism was by immersion of believers, not by sprinkling of infants. A good number of the congregation were of the Mission Covenant Faith, who were all baptized as infants by sprinkling. Thinking this a Pentecostal church, I was not aware that a number of the fine Christians that worshipped there believed that infant baptism was valid and biblical. As I was going on, one of the elder Mission Covenant men suddenly stood to his feet. His face was red as a beet with anger and he declared in a loud voice, "My grandparents and my parents and we were all baptized by sprinkling and if it was good enough for them it is good enough for me." And then he sat down.

I only had this sort of thing happen to me one other time, when I was preaching in a rescue mission to a bunch of alcoholics and street people. I was preaching on the omnipresence of God. In the middle of my sermon a drunk stood up and shouted, "I know where God is. He is in the bathroom upstairs!" He had everyone's attention and proceeded to tell them why he knew that God was in the bathroom upstairs. Apparently his wife had said that morning, "My God, are you still up there?" Everybody burst out in laughter. I had to do some quick thinking to get things back on track. I commended the drunk for his sense of humour, and said that this was not a joking matter and that God was indeed in the bathroom upstairs and everywhere else we may be. He sees and knows who you are and what you are doing. He knows your heart and your needs.

But what could I say to the shocked and silent crowd in that church? I paused for a moment, and then apologized for offending anyone who believed in baptism by sprinkling and went on to complete my sermon. That man and his family left the church. I visited them and asked them to forgive me for my insensitivity, but they did not darken the doors of the church again. The apostle Paul's writing on the marks of a faithful ministry states in 2 Corinthians 6:1–3,

> *As God's fellow workers we urge you not to receive the grace of God in vain. For he says, "In the time of my favour I have heard you, and in the day of salvation I helped you." I tell you, now is the accepted time of God's favour; now is the day of salvation. We put no stumbling block in anyone's path, so that our ministry be not discredited.* (NIV)

My insensibility was a stumbling block to this family which may have discouraged them from accepting God's favour of salvation. I felt badly about that and have wondered how many others may have been offended during the course of our ministry.

New Life Church, Calgary, 1961–1971

I felt a need to upgrade my formal education, so in the spring of 1961 we moved to Calgary so I could attend Mount Royal College. We temporarily moved in with Shirley's folks. Shirley secured a nursing job at the General Hospital. I worked for Nu-west Homes over the summer until the fall semester at Mount Royal College started.

When we arrived in Calgary, Rev. John Watts, Regional Presbyter for the P.A.O.C. churches, asked us to consider taking over a Sunday school that Rev. and Mrs. George Corris had started in the Legion Hall in the community of Ogden. They had recently left Calgary to pastor the church in Cold Lake. Pastor Watts told us that we should work toward planting a branch church in Ogden. The Eighth Avenue Church, under Pastor Watts' leadership, had planted the Montgomery and Capital Hill churches. We accepted this challenge, and later rented a house in Ogden so we could be closer to the people we were trying to minister to. We began that fall with a dozen or so children in the Legion Hall.

We were given the use of the Legion Hall free for two hours each Sunday, starting at 10 a.m. Saturday evening was always a big event at the Legion Hall, until the wee hours of the morning, and nobody cleaned up before the doors were locked. I would get up early Sunday morning to go over to the hall. The stench from the night before was overwhelming: tobacco smoke, liquor, and the awful reek of those who had over-imbibed and thrown up on the floor. The first thing I would do was open all the windows to get rid of the overwhelming smell. The glasses and bottles had to be cleared from the tables, some still partially filled with liquor. Then I had to take down all the tables, mop the floor, and set up some chairs so we could have Sunday school. Some of the women that were helping us as teachers in the Sunday school lived on the North Hill in Calgary. They did not have any way to get to Ogden Sunday mornings, so when I finished the cleaning and setting up I would drive across town to pick them up. Then I had to drive around in Ogden and pick up the children.

The Sunday school grew and we had to have more teachers come to help us. An elderly couple lived across the street from the hall. We started an adult Bible class in their apartment. Soon after, we added a short morning worship service for the teachers and workers and others that joined us from 11:15 a.m. until noon. As well as the Sunday school, we had a midweek Kids' Bible Club in the house we were renting.

By the fall of 1964, the Sunday school attendance, between the children and the adult Bible class and workers, was around eighty. We needed a building of our own.

We had acquired a partially built house, at the end of 22nd Street, which we had finished and were now occupying. Between our home and 78th Avenue, there were five 25-foot lots. Beyond 78th Avenue, there was an eyesore open gravel pit. I inquired about the availability of these five lots for a church building site. I discovered three of the lots belonged to The City of Calgary, and one lot was owned by a Mrs. Dover. She had bought the lot to be a city landowner so she could run for city council. The fifth lot was owned by the Canadian Pacific Railway. These lots were all available to be purchased. The City wanted $250 for each of their lots, but if we purchased all three for a church site, the city would donate one of the three. Mrs. Dover, who was somewhere in Europe on an extended vacation, would also sell her lot for $250. The CPR was not particularly interested in selling. I informed them that we were buying the other lots and would proceed to build around them. They decided to sell, but wanted $365. I had another problem. The land for our church was available, but we did not have the money.

Our first home under construction

I met with the Eighth Avenue church board to inform them that we were ready to plant a church in Ogden and needed to buy land to build a building. Pastor Watts had left Calgary by then to pastor at Broadway Church in Vancouver. Pastor Roy Davis was the new pastor at Eighth Avenue. I went to the church board meeting prepared with all the information and a drawing of the church we planned to build. I discovered that the current church board and pastor seemed to be unaware of the church plant in Ogden. They listened to the presentation and asked me how much I thought it would cost. I told them we could build it with volunteer labour for about $20,000. It would take two thousand hours of volunteer labour to build this church.

Church sod turning ceremony

One of the board members, an engineer with Calgary Power, emphatically and unequivocally stated that it was impossible to build a building of that size for $20,000. He believed it would cost two or three times that, even with volunteer labour. Now who was I to argue with an educated, knowledgeable engineer? The board further informed me that even if they wanted to help me they could not, as the church was in the process of relocating to Elbow Drive and they did not have the money to do both.

Now what was I to do? We had come too far to quit. So we appealed to the PAOC National Office to borrow money from the Pastor's Pension Fund. We were told that we were not eligible for a loan because we did not have an established congregation to repay it.

Church under construction

We then asked the PAOC District for help. The District gave us a $1,000 grant to buy the property. Later, we were able to get a $5,000 loan from the Pension Fund, which the Alberta District signed for. In the spring of 1965, we had a sod-turning and began construction. We decided we would continue to build until we ran out of money.

We never had to quit.

Most of the work was done by volunteers or donated. We bought most of the materials from used lumberyards. The first year, we managed to finish the superstructure. The shingling was completed in a fall snowstorm.

Ogden Church

We moved from the Legion Hall to the completed basement of the church in the fall of 1966. We soon outgrew the basement space, and had to complete the upstairs sanctuary. With God's help, we managed to do the impossible. The compensation board required us to keep a record of all the volunteers and the time they worked on the building. We completed the project within the estimated 2,000-hour projection. We never ran out of funds. The total cost was just over $15,000.

The knowledgeable engineer did not show up as a volunteer, and neither did I inform him that we got it done for less than I had projected. With God, all things are possible. I continued to work in construction and did not take a salary from the church.

During our ten years in Calgary, with God directing our path, we built a house and helped to establish a self-supporting church, all debt-free. We also acquired a lot at Sunnyside Camp and managed to build a cabin so we had somewhere to stay when we were able to attend camp. We did not have Sunday school at the Legion Hall during the summer months, so Shirley and our children were free to be at the camp. I drove up for the weekends.

In 1966, after twelve years of marriage, we took our first real vacation with the family. Shirley's mother had purchased a small holiday tent trailer for us. I took the whole month of August off work, and we went on a camping trip to Los Angeles. On the way, we traveled via Glacier Park, Columbia River, and the Redwood forest. We visited Shirley's Uncle Herb and Aunt Ethel in Kingsburg, California, and my Uncle Asaph and Aunt Mary in Belflower, California. We even went to Disneyland. On our way home, we drove through Utah and visited Yellowstone Park. That was the first of many family camping trips. These were times of bonding and making great memories.

We enjoyed the outdoors, and it was an economical way to vacation. Some campsites were free, but most nights we paid one or two dollars. Since we ate all our meals at the campsites, the food did not cost any more than it would have had we stayed home. Shirley produced amazingly good meals in short order on a two-burner Coleman gas camping stove.

Our youngest daughter, Sharon, arrived on April 16, 1968, at the old Calgary General Hospital, in time for our next family camping adventure.

After our church construction was complete, the congregation wanted me to stop working in construction and be their full-time pastor. I told them I needed a break and that they were to call someone else to be the pastor of the church.

Children's Christmas program, 1970

Our good friend Steve Holomis was chosen in 1969 to be the pastor. We stayed in Calgary for another year, and then moved to Barrhead, Alberta, in February 1971 to be the pastors at Glad Tidings Pentecostal Assembly.

Addition to the Ogden church, mid 1970s

Glad Tidings, Barrhead, Alberta (1971–1974)

My sister Freda had married Eric Kristel, a farmer north of Barrhead. We visited them over Christmas in 1970. Norman Labrentz, the pastor at Glad Tidings church, heard that we would be in Barrhead over the holidays. He asked me to preach on Sunday morning, which I did. I was not aware that Pastor Labrentz was planning on moving to Grand Prairie to pastor a church there. We left Barrhead after the morning service, and stopped to visit my parents in Edmonton on our way back to Calgary. When we arrived in Edmonton, Pastor Labrentz had left a message for us to phone him. We made the call, and he told us that he was leaving Barrhead, and wondered if I would be interested in considering going there to be the pastor of Glad Tidings. After giving this some thought and prayer, we consented to consider this, if the church was interested in having us. Our name was submitted as a candidate. I was asked to come back and preach again, and shortly after that visit we were called to be the pastor.

Glad Tidings Gladtone Singers

Glad Tidings was a delightful church to pastor. The church was full, with a large youth group and a good Sunday school. The church was also blessed with many gifted vocalists and musicians.

During our time there we would often travel with the youth to surrounding towns and community halls to sing and play and share their faith in Christ.

Sunday school record attendance

The church had bought a few lots across the street. It was decided that a pastor's residence should be built on one of these lots. The house was built with volunteer labour, under my supervision. Besides building the house, we were also able to make a number of improvements on the church. We had a mortgage burning and broke all previous Sunday school records with 239 in attendance. I was asked to be Camp Director of Lake Nakanum Pentecostal Camp, and was also elected as Regional Presbyter for the P.A.O.C. churches in the area.

One other thing I desired to see in Barrhead was regular interchurch monthly outreach in the town and community. There were other evangelical churches in Barrhead, and I believed we would all benefit from joint ministry. I spoke to some of the other pastors. The pastor at the Alliance Church was the only one interested. So together we had a monthly outreach in the school auditorium. We showed Christian films and had musical groups come with good crowds in attendance.

Barrhead Church pasonage construction

After we had been in Barrhead two and a half years, I felt God wanted me to move on. I had no reason for feeling this way. Everything in the church was going well. Our oldest, John, had graduated from high school, got his driver's license, bought a car, and left home to work in Edmonton while attending Northwest Bible College. I had the opportunity to buy a lot in Edmonton for a good price, and thought I might take some time out to build a house there. But God had other plans.

Before we went on vacation to BC in August 1973, I informed the church that I would be leaving. I had contacted the British Columbia P.A.O.C. District Superintendent and told him I was contemplating a move and would be interested in a pastorate in BC. The District Superintendent told me the church in Salmon Arm was without a pastor, and he would give them our name.

When we came back from our vacation, the Barrhead church board started to pressure me to stay. Everything was going well, and they questioned why I would want to leave. The thinking in the churches, at that time, was that pastors only left when things were not going well and there was no other option. They asked me if I had another church to go to. I told them no, but that the Salmon Arm Church was without a pastor and might be interested in us. I told the board I needed to make the move before the end of August, before the next school year began. If I did not hear from Salmon Arm before August 15, I would stay another year in Barrhead.

We had a church board meeting on August 15, and I had not heard anything from Salmon Arm. The Barrhead church board was glad to hear the news and I committed myself to be their pastor for another year. The following day, August 16, we heard from the Salmon Arm church. I was being considered as a pastoral candidate. I had to tell them they were one day too late, for I had just committed myself to stay another year in Barrhead.

Barrhead Church mortgage burning—1973

Evangel Church, Thunder Bay (1974–1981)

In the fall of 1973, I received an unexpected phone call from Evangel Church in Thunder Bay, Ontario. The church was without a pastor and they were wondering if I was and interested in coming to Thunder Bay. I told them that I would be making a move, but had committed myself to staying in Barrhead for another year. They said that would not be a problem because they had an interim pastor who would stay until we arrived. I asked them to send me some information about the church and Thunder Bay. I had never heard of Thunder Bay and did not know where it was. The city had just recently undergone a name change. Two cities, Port Arthur and Fort William, had amalgamated with the new name. They sent me the information and, after seeking the Lord for guidance, we felt we should tell them we were willing if it was the will of God for us to go there.

I thought the church in Thunder Bay would go through the usual procedure. We would be asked to come there and preach for a call. The congregation, on their impression of that one sermon, would then decide whether they wanted us. I have always felt this was not a good way to make such an important decision. Every pastor has at least one good sermon. Some pastors cannot preach, but are much loved and are good pastors. I was waiting for an invitation to come to Thunder Bay and preach my best sermon. Instead of an invitation, we received a letter of information. The congregation would be voting on us, sight unseen.

The vote was positive. We were chosen to be the pastor of a church we had not seen, to a congregation of people we had not met, in a city we knew nothing about.

Six months later, on a beautiful July day, we took the daylong drive through beautiful Northern Ontario from Winnipeg to Thunder Bay. We had never been east of Winnipeg. The scenery was magnificent with its many lakes and streams. Just a few miles from Thunder Bay, we came upon Kakabeka Falls, the Niagara Falls of the north. We were overwhelmed by all this splendor.

When we arrived in Thunder Bay, waiting for us was a beautiful church building with a spacious pastor's residence right next door. It appeared that after so many years of struggling to plant and trying to strengthen failing churches, we had now arrived. Here we would be able to concentrate on the ministry of the Word of God and visitation of the saints, and not have to build or upgrade anything.

Old Evangel Church in Thunder Bay – 1974

My, how wrong we were.

The first sermon I preached the first Sunday, I learned later, did not make much of an impression. Some, I am sure, wondered if they had made a mistake in choosing us. When I asked why they had called us sight unseen, I was told that the treasurer of the church had a copy of the book that listed all the ordained pastors of the P.A.O.C. fellowship. As he was going through the book and came upon my name, it just stood out, and he knew that I was the one God wanted to be their pastor. I am sure that probably is not a good way to choose a pastor either. They probably checked our past ministry performance with people who knew us before they made that decision. Besides that, God cared for those in the Thunder Bay church and I know He guided them in their choice.

The church was poised to grow. There were those in the church who sincerely prayed for the church and the city. It was not long before the church was packed and we had to expand to two Sunday morning services. There was not enough room in the church for the Sunday school, so we moved the primary and junior classes to a nearby elementary school. This was only a temporary solution. The church was soon full for the second service. We would have to get a bigger building.

Part of the full church, 1976

We started to search for property, and eventually were able to buy six acres in the inner city area. A 13,000-square-foot building was built by volunteers with a project manager. The project was completed in six months and dedicated in 1979. The new building was evaluated by the bank at over a million dollars. The actual cost was somewhere around $400,000. With the sale of the old church and pastor's residence, we only had a $200,000 bank mortgage. We built the first phase of what would be a multi-phase complex as the church continued to grow. The church has since added a gymnasium.

New Evangel Church

When the pastor's residence was sold to finance the new church building project, I built a new house for our family. I just could not get away from having to build things.

The church had bought a sizable piece of property for a children's summer camp. The property was on the Pole Line Road, not far from Kakabeka Falls, and a creek flowed through it. This camp was initially owned and developed by a service club for a boys and girls camp. The creek had been dammed off to create a swimming area. There was one building on the property. This building had a kitchen and dining area at one end, a meeting hall in the middle, and at the other end housing for the campers. It was used by Evangel Church for their children's camp only one week each year. I thought it should be a regional camp for all the churches in that area, with an enlarged program for perhaps a youth camp and a family camp. The camp soon began to grow as other churches got involved. That meant we needed more housing, and the kitchen needed to be upgraded. We had to build two dorms, one for the girls and one for the boys. The dam over the creek had collapsed and had to be rebuilt. Since I was the only carpenter in the group, they relied on me to draw up the plans and supervise the construction. It was a beautiful site for a camp and was enjoyed by many over the years. The camp has apparently been sold recently. I do not know why.

Centre section of the new church sanctuary

Thunder Bay pastor's new house under construction

Original main building at Little Falls Camp

The Thunder Bay ministerial had been asked to do a daily ten-minute devotional at 5:50 p.m. on the local television station. We were all assigned a week. Most of the pastors could not be bothered, so they would ask me to do it for them. I felt it was an opportunity to declare truths from the Word of God to a TV audience, so I was happy to do it. We would go to the studio one day and do a week of devotionals at a time. The radio station also aired a one-hour, live church service on Sunday mornings at 11:00 a.m., so for a month we were live on the radio from Evangel Church.

Water baptisms were a regular monthly event. People young and old would ask to be baptized and bear witness that they had accepted the Lord Jesus as their Saviour. One Sunday evening, an elderly woman was in the baptismal tank with me. A friend of the elderly lady, sitting in the back row of the overflow, was waving his arms, trying to get my attention. He was pointing to his head. I noticed him and immediately realized his concern. The lady had a beautiful hair piece on, and he was afraid she would lose it when I baptized her, and she would come up out of the water looking like a wet mannequin. I put my left arm behind her back and placed my hand firmly on the wig. She came up out of the water with her hairpiece still in place. I could see the relief on the face of her friend.

Being human, as I am, I am sure I offended people at times. Sometimes things are misconstrued innocently or at times deliberately. One hardy, tall member thought that I had said something negative about his wife. I was making some pastoral calls when I walked inadvertently into a home where there was a "Roast the Pastor Meeting" going on with this man and his wife and members of two other families. I was delighted to see them all. However, it didn't take long for me to learn I wasn't welcome. Prior to this, I was asked by someone about this man's wife's involvement with an independent ministry with no connection to our church, or any other church. My comment was not derogatory. I simply had said I was concerned about people getting involved with groups that are not rooted in a church. They are more prone to fail. I tried to apologize and explain what I had said and what I meant, but the man would not accept my apology. He assured me that if he ever met me in a dark alley, he would certainly teach me a thing or two. I gracefully asked to be excused so that they could carry on with their "Roast the Pastor Meeting."

The people in the Thunder Bay church were very supportive of us as a family. We were in Thunder Bay for nearly seven years. They were busy years, but fruitful.

John graduated from NBC two years after we arrived in Thunder Bay. After his graduation, he married Montreal native Donna Mugford at Evangel in Thunder Bay on July 10, 1976. I asked John to come on staff as my Associate Pastor. John and Donna were a great help and blessing as they took leadership of the youth and children ministry. For a period of time, they produced a children's program for the local TV station. Our first grandson, Evan, was born in Thunder Bay. John and Donna left the church in Thunder Bay to pastor the Portage La Prairie church in Manitoba. Their other two boys, Kyle and Kent, were born in Portage. They moved from Portage to Regina, Saskatchewan, then to Saskatoon where they have been pastoring for many years at Lawson Heights Pentecostal Assembly. John acquired a Masters Degree in Historical Theology at Briercrest College and Seminary. He has served as a professor, as well as the Interim President at Horizon College (formerly Central Pentecostal College). Presently, John is the P.A.O.C. District Superintendent for the Saskatchewan District and the lead pastor of Lawson Heights Church.

Sandra attended Lakehead University and graduated with a Bachelor of Education degree. Sandra had also taken piano lessons from the Roman Catholic sisters at the Catholic Avila Retreat Centre, where she achieved an Associate Diploma from the Western Ontario Conservatory of Music. She attended the Peterborough Pentecostal Bible College, where she met Bob Webster, whom she married in 1983. After their marriage, Bob and Sandra entered the ministry pastoring P.A.O.C. churches in Manitoba, Ontario, Northwest Territories, and Alberta. They have two daughters, Emily and Carissa.

After high school, Glenda studied Social Work at Confederation College in Thunder Bay, graduating in 1979. She went to Central Pentecostal College in Saskatoon for one year, and worked with youth in high schools for Youth for Christ in Edmonton and Winnipeg.

Sharon attended elementary school and part of junior high in Thunder Bay. After graduating from high school in Winnipeg, she went on to study at Central Pentecostal College in Saskatoon, receiving her Diploma in Theology. For years following, Sharon studied and in 2011 achieved a Bachelor of Arts in Religion – Biblical Studies from Rocky Mountain College in Calgary. Sharon met her husband, Terry Froese, through church friends while living in Calgary. They were married in the Rocky Mountains, at Kananaskis, on December 30, 1994. They are the parents of our three youngest grandchildren, Nathaniel, Shailyn, and Grace.

We have been blessed with a total of ten grandchildren, plus two great grandchildren, Noah and Jude, Evan's children.

Much of our families' life took place in Thunder Bay. When it was time to go, again people were asking, "Why are you leaving? Things are going so well. Why do you want to leave?" Those are good, valid questions. I cannot speak for others, but in our case we did not leave any of the churches under duress. We could have stayed and continued to experience growth and the blessing of God on our ministry. Sometimes in retrospect, I think perhaps we always left too soon. Why leave a good church and go to a struggling ministry elsewhere? We were in the ministry because of the calling of God in our life.

I was made a minister, according to the gift of the grace of God given unto me by the effectual working of his power.
—Ephesians 3:7

I thank Christ Jesus our Lord, who hath enabled me, for he hath counted me faithful, putting me in the ministry.
—1 Timothy 1:12

The calling is from God. The enablement to minister is from God. The gifting is from God.

Now there are diversities of gifts but the same spirit.
—1 Corinthians 12:4

He gave some apostles; and some prophets, and some evangelists, and some pastors and teachers.

—Ephesians 4:11

Our gifting was that of church planting. I felt more comfortable starting a church than keeping a church running after it was started, or in some cases restarted. That was my gifting. I have been asked for the key or keys to our success. I do not know. You will have to ask God how He somehow enabled us to do it. I didn't have any keys, I just went wherever God would have me to go, and endeavored to do whatever He wanted me to do.

We left Thunder Bay to go to a small church that was in turmoil in Winnipeg. I would like to think that pastors, in most instances, at the prompting of the Holy Spirit, leave one church to go to another because their particular gifting and callings are needed elsewhere. It is their callings and gifting that determine their place and field of ministry, like Philip in Acts 8:26, Peter in Acts 10, and Paul in Acts 16:9–10. God directs those He has chosen for the ministry in a variety of ways.

Sherwood Assembly: Winnipeg, Manitoba. (1981–1986)

We moved from Thunder Bay to Winnipeg in 1981. I was elected as Presbyter for the Winnipeg and surrounding area churches. The Sherwood Church had been pioneered by Rev. Bob Hoover. The next pastor that followed him after a few years was faced with a crisis and had to resign. I felt that God wanted us to go there.

The church had a good number of young people and good children's ministry. During our four years of ministry there, the church stabilized and experienced some growth.

While in Winnipeg, Shirley took a nurses refresher course and went back to work. However, she became ill and was hospitalized for several months. I did not do any construction work in our four years in Winnipeg.

Interior of the Sherwood Assembly, Winnipeg

One of the highlights during our ministry in Winnipeg was the visit of an African Church leader as a guest speaker at the Sherwood Church. He shared with the church what God was doing in Africa. Everyone enjoyed his ministry. At the end of the service, he sat down and I was in the process of closing the service when he interrupted me, and said he had something else he should do.

So I gave him the microphone again. He asked the congregation, "How many of you would like to see your pastor go to Africa?" Of course, everyone raised their hands. He then said, "All of you who raised hands, it is going to cost you something. The fare to Africa is $1,800 and we will look after him while he is there. We need eighteen people to give $100 so your pastor can come to Africa. Raise your hand if you would like to give $100 so your pastor can come to Africa. In two minutes, he had made it possible for us to make a missions trip to Africa. This we did a year later.

On the way to Africa, Shirley and I had a one-day stopover in Israel and another day on our way back. We were able to spend a day in the old City of Jerusalem, visited the garden of Gethsemane, and the Garden tomb and other sites. On the way back we took a day bus trip to the Sea of Galilee. In Africa, we ministered in Kenya and Tanzania. We were able to visit the Gobi Animal Reserve, swam in the Indian Ocean, and saw and experienced much more on our three weeks in Africa. There were dozens of other churches in Winnipeg that this African church leader could have gone to. He came to the Sherwood Church, and not only blessed the church with his ministry but also Shirley and me with a trip we could only dream of. I think it was God's way of paying us back for the years we could not afford to take trips or vacations.

One of the other highlights in our stay in Winnipeg was Bob and Sandra's wedding, on May 14, 1983, at the Sherwood Church.

My siblings and I in the summer of 1986.
Left to right: Adeline, Sefrin, Reinhart, Reubin, Freda, Bennard

Calvary Temple: Brandon, Manitoba (1986–1987)

In 1986, we were asked by the District Superintendent if we would go to Brandon, Manitoba. The pastor at Calvary Temple was asked to leave, which created some turmoil in the church. The church needed someone to come there on a short-term basis to calm the waters. They thought I might be able to do that. I consented to go.

Brandon Calvary Temple

Glenda had been hired to be the administrator at Bethel Christian Assembly in Brandon, Manitoba. She got to know Michael Edworthy, who was a computer engineering technologist. When she introduced Michael to us, I had some doubt as to Michael's choice for a lifelong occupation. I did not know much about computers at that point, and still don't, so I wondered if being a computer engineering technologist was going to be a viable occupation. Otherwise, he seemed to be a nice enough young man and Glenda was old enough to make up her own mind. And she did. The wedding was at the Bethel church on October 4, 1986. Computer technology has proven to be a good choice for Michael, and Michael has been a good choice for Glenda.

So she could be with us before Michael and Glenda's wedding, Shirley's seventy-nine-year-old mother flew from Calgary to Brandon a week early. The day she arrived in Brandon, on Friday, she had a heart attack while she was sitting with us at the supper table. We phoned the ambulance and she was rushed to the hospital. She seemed to be alright each time we visited. Early on Sunday morning, we received a call from the hospital informing us that Mom had passed away. Sharon went to Brandon from Saskatoon to help Glenda and Michael with wedding details, while the rest of the family drove to Calgary for the funeral. We, including extended family, made it back to Brandon in time for the Friday evening wedding rehearsal and Saturday wedding at the Bethel Pentecostal Church.

It was a good year for the Calvary Temple church. The church had recovered from the turmoil of the previous year, and was ready to call a pastor. They were able to do their traditional annual Singing Christmas Tree program to packed crowds for several nights. We were no longer needed, but stayed till they had completed the process of choosing a new pastor.

The Singing Christmas Tree

Carman, Manitoba: (1988–1992)

When we left Brandon, we did not have another church to go to, so we moved to Portage La Prairie where our son John was the Pastor at Highway Tabernacle. We rented a beautiful 100-year-old house. Sharon was attending C.P.C. Bible College in Saskatoon, Saskatchewan, so there were just the two of us, Shirley and me. I got a construction job with a company building a grocery store, a McDonald's restaurant, and a couple of MAC's Convenience Stores in Portage.

The elderly pastor, Rev. Hamilton, of the Carman Pentecostal Church, was in the hospital dying with cancer. The Carman church was one of the oldest congregations in the district. It was a vibrant, thriving church in the '30s and '40s, but had continued to decline to the point where there were only a few people left. The old building they were worshiping in had been built in 1890 by a Baptist group. The Pentecostals purchased the church in the early 1930s, and very little had been done to improve the building. Pastor Hamilton was pastor of the church for a number of years before he retired at sixty-five. Pastor Hamilton and his wife had a house in Carman and planned to retire there. Because the congregation was small and the church building was old at the time of Pastor Hamilton's retirement, the district could not find a replacement pastor right away. Since Pastor Hamilton lived in Carman, the district asked him to look after things until a replacement could be found. Years slipped by and no replacement could be found for the Carman church. The retired Pastor Hamilton faithfully did what he could to keep the doors open.

With Pastor Hamilton dying in the hospital, the district faced a dilemma: "What shall we do about the Carman church?" The conclusion was there is nothing else we can do but close the church since we cannot find a pastor to go there. I was on the district executive and I was not in favour of closing the church. It was the only non-ethnic evangelical church in the community of approximately five thousand people. I said we should try to keep the church open. Then they asked me, "Are you willing to go there?"

I really did not have anything else to do at the time, as the construction job had come to an end, so I said, "Sure I'll go there."

Then they asked me, "Will you stay there for at least one year?"

I told them, "It will take more than a year for me to get to know the community and the community to get to know me. I'll stay as long as it takes to get the church back on its feet and running again."

We bought a building lot in Carman and made arrangements with a company in Morden to build a prefab house for us. At first while the house was being built we just drove out to Carman from Portage La Prairie for the Sunday service. We moved to Carman in the summer of 1988. I knew we had to make some improvements to the old church building before we could expect people to come to worship there. We needed better washroom facilities, a larger foyer, a nursery, a church office, and a pastor's study. I drew up a renovations improvement plan for the building and submitted it to the town for approval, which they were happy to give, for the church had been an eyesore for a long time. The PAOC District Executive also granted their approval.

In the spring, I had a bulldozer come and knock down the small entrance to the old building, and excavate a basement for the new addition. The new addition, built with volunteer help in Carman and some from Winnipeg, would double the size of the building. The construction of the new addition got the attention of the community. I'm sure many people wondered what was going on at the Pentecostal church, as they had thought it was going to be closed.

The new addition to the old building

Carman is a small town and the news of new life at the church soon spread throughout the entire community. To further grab the attention of the community, I got permission from the high school to use the school auditorium one Sunday evening a month, for special events. We showed Dobson Family Films and had musical groups like choirs, male quartets, and the Continental Singers come to bless the community. We entered floats in the Carman Fair parade. All these activities raised awareness for us, and with the new look of the addition to the old building, people started to come and see what we were all about.

The parade float at the Carman Fair

Within four years, the church was full again and it was time to call another pastor and for us to retire, as my sixty-fifth birthday was coming up. The District Superintendent shook his head. "I don't know what it is about you, Reubin, but you seem to succeed everywhere you go."

I said, "I don't know either."

"Except the Lord build the house, they labour in vain that build it" (Psalm 127:1). When I responded to the call of God to the ministry, I told the Lord, "I'll go where you want me to go. I'll do what you want me to do. But please Lord, I can't do it alone. You have to help me." If I have had any measure of success, it is because the Lord helped us, and all the glory belongs to Him. I suppose the work ethic of the homestead, where we worked from sunrise to sunset everyday and thought nothing of it, may have had something to do with it as well.

The Carman church continued to grow. The congregation was able to acquire three acres of land at the edge of the town, and has built a new and much bigger church with a thriving congregation.

With God, all things are possible.

The new church building

Part of the crowd at the new church dedication

While we were in Carman, I was asked to supervise a workforce group of twenty-seven people going to Argentina to transform a large warehouse into a church. We had to add an addition to the warehouse for washrooms, besides refinishing the floor and painting. Some of the group did some tract distribution and the pastors in the group preached on Sunday and during the week. At the end of our time in Argentina, we took a bus trip to see the spectacular Iguasu Falls on the Parana River bordering Argentina, Paraguay, and Brazil. The Parana River is South America's second-largest and longest river, and it flows into the Atlantic Ocean about twenty kilometers north of Buenos Aires. Our organizers also planned a river trip to the Tigre Delta Island in the Parana River Delta. In the River Delta, which is 14,000 square kilometers, there are thousands of islands with 25,000 island dwellers. Of course, there are no roads or bridges, only piers for boats. There are no stores, only boats laden with food supplies and clothing, and everything else needed by the island dwellers. No shopping trip to the malls there; only a short walk to the pier. There are no school buses, only school boats that pick up the children at each pier for school. Many of the island dwellers never leave the River Delta. Some islands have a church where people come to worship in their boats. We visited one of these churches that would seat about two hundred people.

Iguasu Falls

The islands are wooded, teeming with a great variety of birds. The island dwellers grow the food they need on the rich island soil. They have fruit trees and market the fruit for income. Some islands are small and may have only one, or a few families on them, while others are quite large with a good community of residents. The weather in that region is quite moderate, so one can bathe in the river year round so there probably is no need for a bathtub or shower in the homes. It was an interesting and informative trip that we all enjoyed.

We accomplished a lot in the two weeks we were in Argentina. Due to a slump in the economy, there were many empty warehouses for sale. The churches were experiencing great growth and needed places for the people to worship and were buying the warehouses and renovating them for places of worship. We were glad that we had the opportunity and privilege of helping one church to have a place to worship.

Putting the roof on the washroom addition to the warehouse church

Retirement and New Opportunities (1992–Present)

It was time to retire. But where? We had lived in twelve different places, and moved twenty-two times over the course of forty-seven years of ministry. We made so many moves because in most places we first found temporary accommodations, and then later were able to find, buy, or build suitable housing. We had become attached to all the places we had lived. In the end, Alberta was the logical choice. Most of our relatives and former friends were living here. Glenda and Michael and Sharon were living in Calgary, so we chose Calgary.

When we arrived in Calgary, we first rented an apartment in the Beddington area of northwest Calgary.

Evangel Church, in the southeast community of Forest Lawn, was without a pastor. This was a relatively new congregation pioneered in 1984 by Rev. Ed and Kathy Pahl. At first, they had rented a number of different locations for their services. Then in 1990 the congregation was able to buy a strip mall on Hubalta Road. They set aside one area in the mall for the church, and the rest was rented out to various tenants. This was a huge venture for a small congregation. There was much work to be done to renovate the mall for a church, and a lot of money was needed for the furnishings they needed. Two of the members had signed over their homes to the bank for security for the mortgage. Others gave sacrificially, not only money, but of their time to prepare the church for a meeting place. The congregation moved into the partially renovated building and the attendance increased.

Evangel Christian Assembly, Forest Lawn, Calgary

Pastor Pahl was a strong leader and a good example. I'm told he got right in there and got his hands dirty with all the rest of the congregation. The church was well-managed under his leadership and they felt the impact of his absence when he resigned and moved to the British Columbia coast to be involved in a television ministry.

Pastor Pahl's successor did not seem to have the leadership skills or ministry gifting that were needed by the church at this point in their history. During this time, the rental space in the building was difficult for the congregation to manage. The size of the congregation also started to dwindle. Soon bills were unable to be paid and it was difficult to keep up on building maintenance. The eleven rooftop furnaces desperately needed repairs. The roof leaked, and buckets were hung in the tiled ceiling to catch the water when it rained. The bank was threatening foreclosure if the mortgage arrears weren't paid. The pastor resigned when the church was unable to pay his salary.

Sarah Siemons, a retired seasoned pastor, was attending the church at the time. She willingly stepped forward to temporarily fill the gap and keep the church going. When the church board discovered we were in Calgary, they appealed to us for help. We were available to give the required leadership. We agreed to do what we could to salvage the building and the congregation.

God's plan for the church is that every church should have a pastor to lead them. It is unfortunate when churches have to function at times without a pastor, or when pastors lack the giftings needed for that particular church to grow. Being a pastor is a high and holy calling that requires commitment on our part and giftings from God.

The Apostle Peter wrote to pastors about their responsibilities:

Be shepherds of God's flock that is under your care, serving as overseers—not because you must, but because you are willing, as God wants you to be, not greedy for money, but eager to serve; not lording it over those entrusted to you, but being examples to the flock.
—1 Peter 5:2–3, NIV

The Apostle Paul also wrote to the leaders in the church:

Keep watch over yourselves and all the flock of which the Holy Spirit has made you overseers. Be shepherds of the church of God, which He bought with His own blood. I know that after I leave, savage wolves will come among you and will not spare the flock.
—Acts 20:28–29, NIV

We were told in Bible School that the pastor's chimney should be the first to smoke in the morning. That was when wood burning stoves were used for both cooking and to heat the house. The smoke from the chimney let the whole community know that the pastor was up and at it. Our upbringing on the farm also taught us if something was broken, fix it. If something needed doing, do it. Don't ignore it or wait for someone else to come along.

Prize float in the Forest Lawn Parade

Unfortunately, as in every occupation, there are pastors who have not acquired the work ethic and leadership skills needed in caring for a flock or a building. Every church is different and requires unique ministry to succeed. Pastors must be willing and able to adapt to provide the ministry the church needs.

The ministry is work. Paul's words to the church in Ephesians 4:11–12 is that God gave to the church pastors and teachers for the *"work"* of the ministry. In writing to Timothy, Paul admonishes him to do the *"work"* of the ministry. The ministry is work, and the pastor has to be an example. If the pastor does not work, neither will the people.

The prophet Jeremiah said, *"A curse on him who is lax in doing the Lord's work!"* (Jeremiah 48:10, NIV)

When Evangel asked for our help, I told them I would not expect or accept any pay until the bills were all paid and the renovations completed. The people immediately rallied and we had regular work bees to fix the furnaces and leaky roof. The congregation began to grow again and money began to flow. Within a year, the bills were all paid and there was money in the bank. The church was salvaged to continue its ministry to the multitude of lost and hurting souls in southeast Calgary.

It was now time to call another pastor for the church, and we could return to retirement. When we accepted the challenge of helping Evangel Church get back on its feet, we bought a house in the community of West Dover so we could be closer to the church. We have been a part of Evangel Church for the past twenty years.

After the year of rebuilding Evangel, we were available for ministry in other places when someone was needed. We were able to fill in at Vulcan, Pincher Creek, Turner Valley, and Canmore. I did some basement renovations, and Shirley did some nursing. We had bought a 24-foot Argosy holiday trailer and a used Cadillac to pull the trailer. We were now able to take extended vacations in comfort. We were able to drive to California along the west coast and to Mexico. We also drove to Alaska with my brother Reinhart and his wife Deloris. We bought a timeshare, and for a number of years were able to stay in luxurious resorts in places like Florida, Grand Bahamas, Jamaica, California, Philippines, Hawaii, Idaho, Missouri, and Mexico.

Vacationing in the luxury of an Airstream

God somehow rewarded us for all the years we missed vacationing while others seemed to be able to do it. God is truly no man's debtor. He sees the sacrifices we make, and He will somehow repay. The hymn writer expresses it so well:

> *It pays to serve Jesus, it pays every day, it pays every step of the way, though the pathway to glory may sometimes be drear, you'll be happy each step of the way.*
>
> —Frank C. Huston

Missions Ministry Opportunities

In 1995, a Canadian evangelist asked me to go to Albania to be part of the Evangelistic Team for a five-day crusade the first week of June. I would join him in Durres, a major coastal city of 100,000 people. I was to be there for the crusade and would stay after to do the follow-up and establish a church. The crusade was held in the stadium with about two thousand in attendance. The evangelist had acquired 20,000 New Testaments, in the Albanian language of Shqip, to be handed out during the crusade. At the end of the first evening meeting, it was announced that we had a Shqip New Testament for everyone who wanted one. There didn't seem to be any way to orderly form a line or lines for the distribution of the Bibles. The crush was so dense that it was impossible to distribute the New Testaments. It was decided that they would be left for me to distribute after the crusade was over.

Albania is in the Macedonia region where the Apostle Paul went to preach the gospel after he had a vision of the Macedonian man praying for him to come there and preach (Acts 16:9–13). The old Roman road and bridges that the Apostle Paul walked on in his response to that call nearly two thousand years ago are still there. Albania was greatly influence by the Apostle Paul, and others. It was known as a Christian region, until the Muslim Turks invaded in the 1400s. The Albanians told us that Christianity was eliminated by executing anyone who professed to be a believer in Christ Jesus. For over four hundred years it was a Muslim region, until the communists seized control in 1944 and outlawed all religions. A general strike in 1991 weakened the Communist Party. On March 22, 1992, in a general election, the Communist government was toppled by the Democratic Party, and missionaries were able to enter Albania again and preach the gospel.

20,000 New Testaments

The Kosovo region on the northern border of Albania is populated by Albanians who speak the Shqip language. While the communists were in control in Albania, missionaries were working in Kosovo printing Christian Bibles and books in preparation to enter Albania when the doors would again be open. They were ready when it happened in 1992. When we arrived in Durres in 1995, there were Christian tracts and books available for distribution. We not only had those 20,000 New Testaments, but also 10,000 colourful books for children on the life of Jesus entitled *The Road to Heaven*.

There were two dialects of the Shqip language spoken in Albania: Geg in the north, and Tosk in the south. In 1972, the communists standardized the language and prohibited the people from speaking anything but the standardized Shqip, and from learning any other languages.

10,000 colourful copies of the children's book The Way to Heaven

After the communist regime collapsed, the whole world came to help Albania rebuild. After over forty years of neglect by the communists and four hundred years by the Muslims, everything had to be rebuilt: roads, schools, hydro transmission, hospitals, the harbour, etc. The consultants, architects, engineers, and others who came to help all spoke English and needed interpreters. Any Albanian who spoke any English was immediately snatched up. When we arrived in 1995, I needed an interpreter, but there was no one available.

Education was not compulsory in Albania, and it was the parents' responsibility to see that their children attended school. Most of the parents had to work, so the children were on their own. If they felt like it, they would go to school; if not, they would roam the streets. Genti was one of those children who did not attend school very often. His father was a policeman, and his mother sold vegetables at the market. He managed to get through the fifth grade. In his early teens, he was like a hippie roaming the streets of Tirana, the capital city. The Victory Church was doing ministry in Tirana, and Genti accepted the Lord. This church had started a Bible school, and Genti enrolled, as he really did not have much else to do. All the lectures at the Bible school were given in English and interpreted into Shqip. In a year, Genti learned enough English from listening to the teachers that one could have a conversation with him. Genti, an eighteen-year-old hippie type, was hired to be my interpreter.

I was accustomed to speaking with interpreters in Africa, Argentina, and ethnic churches in Canada. With a good interpreter, everything flows smoothly, and there are no hesitations. Genti took pride in the fact that he had learned to speak English in one year. I told him that I have spoken English for over sixty years and still did not know English that well. I had to write out my sermon or Bible study word-for-word and go over it very carefully with Genti to make sure he knew what I was talking about.

Genti would often say, "There is no word for that in the Shqip language."

I would respond, "Genti, for every English word there is a Shqip word. You just don't know it yet."

I had purchased an English-Shqip dictionary, so I would look up the word in the dictionary and show it to him. He would look at it and finally nod and say, "Okay." When we spoke with Genti interpreting, I was never quite certain he had remembered the word I had just taught him. With his 5th grade education in Shqip, I am sure he even had a very limited vocabulary in the Shqip language.

When the communist government seized control in Albania in 1944, they outlawed all religions. The Albanians had no religious history for three generations. They had never had a Bible in their hand or sung a hymn in their life, so we had to keep things very basic and simple. Genti's year at Bible school helped because he already knew and understood the basics of the gospel.

After the crusade was over and the evangelist returned to Canada, Genti and I were left living in a bedbug-infested room the evangelist had rented for us to stay in during the crusade. He had also arranged for a young Albanian couple to work with us after the crusade was over. The husband had a small keyboard that he played rather poorly. He was to be the musician in our church planting endeavor. The husband could not speak any English, the wife only some. We needed a place for the four of us to live. The bedbug-infested house did not have room for four people. A missionary couple from Holland was going back home for a month's vacation, and they did not want to leave their home unattended. They needed someone to house-sit. We took our stuff and the 20,000 New Testaments and temporarily moved there. Before the month was over, we were able to rent a spacious two-bedroom home on the upper floor of a two-storey newly built apartment. It had a bathroom with a toilet, shower and hot water—novelties in Albania.

Kitchen shelves we built for pots, pans, food and dishes

The apartment was unfurnished. This was a problem. We needed everything from dishes, pots and pans, and utensils, to appliances, kitchen cupboards, and bedroom and living room furniture. I didn't have a car and did not know where I would find the supplies we needed. I had befriended the Kammers, a missionary couple from Germany. Hartmuth Kammer helped me, and we were able to find what we needed. We were ready to move in before the Dutch couple returned from their vacation. On moving day, we hired a dray man who had a team of horses and a wagon. We loaded our things and the 20,000 New Testaments on the wagon and moved across town to our new apartment.

I was able to rent the lower floor of a two-storey restaurant for our Sunday morning worship service. We'd move the tables aside and set up chairs for the service. I soon learned that the Albanian musician was more of a liability than an asset and had to tell him we did not need his musical gifts. We gave him an extra month's pay and sent him and his wife on their way. His wife was a good housekeeper and cook—we could have used her.

The two-storey restaurant

I tried to do the follow-up of the 250-some people who had filled out decision cards during the crusade. The Albanians did not seem to have any addresses. The addresses that were given were incomplete or incorrect, so we could not make contact with them. So Genti and I would go out on the street, with backpacks full of Shqip New Testaments. In each Bible we placed a printed invitation and information slip with the time and place of our Sunday service. At first we had around a half-dozen people come to our Sunday morning service at the restaurant.

The Kammers, the German missionary couple, lived in Durres. They had come to Albania to do ministry with the children in the surrounding villages. School was from 8:00 a.m. until noon, Monday to Friday. In the afternoons, the children were free. The Kammers went to two villages a day, five days a week. They would be in one village from 1:00 to 2:30 p.m., then drive to another village for a second children's meeting from 4:00 to 5:30 p.m. They were gifted children's ministry workers. Mrs. Kammer and their teenage daughter were very talented musicians, both on the keyboard and guitars. They had also taken in some needy teenage girls. The Kammers decided to join us in our service at the restaurant on Sunday mornings. What a blessing their music was, and they were able to have a children's feature in the service. The Kammers' involvement made the restaurant service something the people enjoyed. We preached a simple gospel message and encouraged the people to accept Jesus Christ as their Saviour. In three months, we had a congregation of sixty and our first water baptismal service. We baptized thirty-five new converts in the Adriatic Sea.

Water baptism in the Adriatic Sea

The Kammers asked me to come with them to the villages. They said they knew how to minister to the children, but needed to reach the adults in these villages with the gospel and did not know how to do that. I declined. I told them there were 100,000 people in Duress to reach and I just did not have the time to come to the villages with them. They would not accept my answer. So, eventually I told them I would go with them but only for three days a week, Monday through Wednesday.

Sunday morning service in the Durres restaurant

In the villages, we paid someone a dollar or two to rent their living room for a couple hours. The rooms were wall-to-wall people, mostly youth, and they listened intently to the Word of God. Some of the workers involved in the ministry there today are converts who came to those village meetings. A church was eventually built in one of those villages.

Wall-to-wall people for a Bible study

One day, a couple of young men came to one of our village meetings. They listened for a little while and then started to create a disturbance, saying that what we were telling them was all a bunch of lies. I told them, in my sweet gentle way, that we were studying the Word of God and they were welcome to stay and listen. I asked them to please leave if they could not quietly listen. They left. As they were leaving, they said something to Genti.

After the meeting I asked Genti what they had said. They had told him, "We'll kill you!" I asked Genti if he thought they meant it and if they would be able to do that. In Albania, then and still perhaps today, you could get away with murder.

Genti's father needed heart surgery in Tirana. On the day the surgery was scheduled, I told Genti to go to Tirana and be with his family. When he came home, I asked him how the surgery had gone. He said the doctor did not do the surgery and had put it off until the next week. It happened again the next week. The doctor postponed the surgery for another week. On the third week, it happened again. The doctor was waiting for the family to give him some extra money before he did the surgery. This time Genti's uncle told the doctor that if he did not do the surgery the next week, he would kill him. Killing the heart doctor did not sound like a good idea to me. Then who would do the surgery?

I asked Genti if his uncle could actually kill the doctor. He replied that he could and would. I wanted to know what would happen to Genti's uncle if he killed the doctor. Genti said that murder was not a problem in Albania. The family would just get some money together and pay the judge and his uncle would be released.

The next week, Genti went to be with his family on the day of the surgery. Again, the doctor postponed and rescheduled. Genti's uncle took a knife and stabbed the doctor. Fortunately, it was not a mortal wound. However, the doctor now was a patient in the same hospital as Genti's father. They transferred his father to a hospital in another city. His uncle ended up in prison. The family got some bribe money together and his uncle was released. We left Albania shortly after that and do not know if Genti's father ever had the surgery. I do know he died a few years later.

Genti was very quiet on our next trip to the village where he had been threatened by the two young men. They didn't come back to fulfill their threat, and Genti continued to be my interpreter.

Albania was, and probably still is, a very backward, poverty-stricken nation. While there, we saw farmers plowing their fields with oxen. Oxen yoked to heavily laden wagons. Donkeys were used to transport things. Farmers worked their fields with hand tools. There were ancient traditions, like vengeance killings. If one accidentally or intentionally killed someone, the family who lost the loved one was traditionally obliged to avenge the death, killing someone in the family responsible for the death. If it was an accidental death and vengeance was taken, then the innocent family was obligated to avenge the vengeance death. In this process sometimes entire families would be liquidated.

Plowing the field with oxen

Oxen pulling a heavy load

I realized I would not be able to stay in Albania for the long term needed, and that I did not have the resources this growing ministry would need to continue to grow. I appealed to the evangelist who brought me to Albania, but he did not respond. I knew he would not be able to help. I contacted the P.A.O.C. missions department. They said they were sorry but they could not help because they had already overextended themselves and could not take on another project.

What could I do? Here I was in a ripened mission field with the doors wide open, and there were no reapers and no one seemed to be able to help or to care. Jesus said, *"The harvest truly is great, but the labourers few; pray ye therefore the Lord of the harvest, that he would send forth labourers into his harvest"* (Luke 10:2).

We needed help; we prayed and the Lord sent labourers.

Village children meeting

The Nehemiah Pentecostal group in Germany had come to Albania earlier, and had established successful ministries in the eastern regions of Albania. I contacted them and told them what we were doing. I told them I would not be staying in Albania for very long and I needed someone to take over when I left. I asked if we could affiliate the work with the Nehemiah Mission. They willingly assumed responsibility for the church and ministries in Durres and the surrounding villages.

Durres Gypsy Church

Shirley joined me our last few months in Albania. We left in March 1996, after doing ministry there for nearly a year. The work under the leadership of the Nehemiah Fellowship has continued to grow. They have baptized over one hundred new converts each year and have built a big ministry centre in Durres. They now have twenty full-time workers in Durres ministering to over 1,500 people in thirty-five weekly meetings. Their ministry includes children's meetings, youth gatherings, women's Bible studies, and others. They also have an annual children's camp at a seashore location. A ministry in the Gypsy section of the city of Duress was started when we were in Durres. This is now a well-established ministry with its own building. They still consider me the founder of this ministry, although I only played a small role in what is now a reputable, ongoing ministry in the city of Durres and its surrounding villages.

When we returned from Albania to Calgary, we found Evangel Church was again in dire straits. The church funds were depleted, and the pastor had to leave. They appealed to me again for help. I again donated my time in ministry to the church for another year. At the end of the year, 1998, the church asked our son-in-law Rev. Robert Webster and his wife Sandra, our daughter, to come and pastor the church. Under the Webster's fifteen-year leadership, the church has remained stable with an effective ministry.

We have been with Evangel church for more than twenty years. When we were not serving as interim pastors, we served where we were needed. My carpenter skills have always been needed in maintenance and occasional renovations projects. The church has had an effective ministry to seniors over the past twenty-two years. We've always been involved in this outreach to seniors in the community and the church. For ten years, we gave leadership to this delightful group. Our age and physical limitations have made it impossible to continue in this role.

Over the years since our retirement, we have had a number of ministry opportunities. In October 1997, I was asked to go to the Ukraine to do ten days of lectures in a Bible school in Teranopul. At the end of the ten days, I went to Kolosna, Ukraine, where my parents grew up. I had the privilege of preaching in a Ukrainian Baptist church on a Sunday morning, one hundred years after my grandfather had preached in the German Baptist churches in that region. In February 2001, we ministered in Manila and the Northern Province of the Philippines. In 2003, I was asked to be part of three regional convocations in Southern India. Our experiences abroad made us realize that God was moving by His Spirit all over the world. *"The harvest truly is great but the labours are few"* (Luke 10:2). The words of the chorus express it so well:

> *All over the world the Spirit is moving.*
> *All over the world as the prophet said it would be,*
> *Deep down in my heart there's a mighty revelation*
> *Of the Glory of the Lord as the waters cover the sea.*
> —Roy Turner

We feel honored that God called us and enabled us to do the work of the ministry.

South India Crusade—1997

Where Does the Story of Me End?

We grew up and lived in an amazing period in the history of humanity. We witnessed the explosion of technology and knowledge, the beginning of space travel, and exploration of the universe. Radio was an amazing thing; being able to pick voices out of the air miles from nowhere in the bush in Northern Alberta. When we told our father that soon we could have a device that would take pictures out of the air to be seen on a box screen in our homes, he said that is impossible. How are they going to be able to do that? When he later watched on television as the first man stepped out of the lunar lander onto the moon, he could not believe it and said it could not be real. The current generation with their cell phones, iPods, and countless other devices take the cyber world for granted. It wasn't that long ago when these things didn't exist and couldn't even be imagined.

We have lived through horrific wars and the brutality of dictators and demagogues. We have also seen the outpouring of love and compassion of those who care. Personally, I'm amazed at how far we have come: from poverty stricken, uneducated, barefooted homesteaders to sophisticated city dwellers, with the next generation of educated, degreed descendants; from a two-roomed log house with no amenities in the woods, to spacious well-furnished luxurious homes on beautifully landscaped city lots; from horse and wagon on trails through the bush, to expensive shiny automobiles speeding on paved highways. How did it all happen? Well I'm sure that some of it is due to hard work. I think most of it is due to the blessing of God on our family.

The blessing of the Lord, it maketh rich and addeth no sorrow with it.
—Proverbs 10:22

Seek ye first the kingdom of God, and his righteousness; and all these things shall be added unto you.
—Matthew 6:33

Yes, it pays to serve Jesus. It pays every day and every step of the way.

When my father Emil was courting my mother Alvina and they fell in love, my father had to get permission from my grandfather, Julius Hein, to marry my mother. I do not know what the outcome would have been if Julius had not granted that permission. My father and mother were both committed Christians, and sought the Lord for guidance in choosing their life companions. With God's help, they made the right choices. They were blessed with six wonderful children, including me.

Shirley tells me she prayed that God would bring the right person into her life, and she is convinced that person was me. I did not ask permission or consult anyone when I proposed to Shirley. I knew she was God's choice for me. Perhaps if I had asked her father for permission I might have been out of the picture in short order.

When our children were growing up, as parents we were concerned about the person they would choose to marry. I am glad they did not ask for permission, except for Terry. If they had, I probably would have rejected the spouses they married because I was convinced that no one would be good enough for our children.

In October of 1994, Terry had made arrangements for us—Sharon, Shirley and me—to vacation with him and his parents in Puerto Vallarta, Mexico, for a week. One evening, Terry asked me to go for a walk with him on the beach. As we walked he told me that he loved Sharon and wanted my permission to marry her. Trying to convince me that he was the one for Sharon, Terry made a lot of promises and told me he would be good to her. After such a speech, I could hardly say, "No way, go away, get lost."

I'm sure if I had, they would have done it anyway. So I just said, "Sure, go ahead and take her," or something like that. When we returned from our walk and sat on the beach with the waves gently lapping the shore, the setting sun reflected on the rolling ocean waves, Terry knelt down before Sharon and opened an engagement ring box and proposed to her. Now that's the way it should be done, not like my proposal to Shirley in the cramped front seat of a small, rusty, borrowed Austin car on a crowded dimly lit parking lot.

Terry's beach proposal to Sharon

I am amazed at how well-suited each of our children's life companions are for each one of them. We love them all. Shirley has been a wonderful life companion. She has graciously tolerated all my blunders. She has cooked remarkably good meals even when the cupboard was bare. She was a loving, patient, wise, caring mother for our children. Thank you, Shirley, for being so good and kind to me. You have gently and patiently been refining me from a crude, barefooted homesteader woodsman to what I am today. I know there is still room for improvement.

I have deliberately avoided putting many people's names in this story. One reason is that I have never been good at remembering names, and secondly, I did not want to embarrass anyone. This story is as I remember my life experience. There are other things I remember that I could have included. Then there are things that I should have included, but I cannot remember them.

As I write this, Shirley and I are near our mid-eighties. We realize our days are numbered. I am living in a senior's manor and Shirley has spent most of this year, 2013, in the hospital. She is now living in a Seniors Extended Care Facility. The years have gone by so quickly. Jesus said,

> *Lay not up for yourselves treasures upon earth, where moth and rust doth corrupt, and where thieves break through and steal; but lay up for yourselves treasures in heaven, where neither moth nor rust doth corrupt, and where thieves do not break through and steal. For where your treasure is, there will your heart be also.*
> —Matthew 6:19–21

God has given us life, and we have tried to live it according to His plan and purposes.

Has it been worth it all? What have we received for our efforts? Stuff! As we take stock of what we have received, we discover we are blessed beyond measure. When we had to downsize to move into the manor, we discovered we had so much to dispose of. Ads on Kijiji, two garage sales, and oodles of giveaways—it seemed we'd never get rid of it all. We did not! We eventually had to hire a junk trucker, who for the money we made at the garage sales hauled the rest of the stuff to the dump. These were all our earthly treasures. Of course, there was a time when we needed these things, but in the end it is useless and burdensome.

What treasures do we have at the end of our lifetime? If someone were to ask me to list three things I possess and cherish most at the end of my life, I would have to say "Family! Family! Family!" We have been blessed with a wonderful family, both in-laws and out-laws. (Out-laws are the family members of the in-laws.)

There are also the many people who were so kind and good to Shirley and me over the years. These friends we cherish. Everything else really does not matter much now.

Yes, it pays to serve Jesus! It is true:

Only one life to live 'twill soon be past,
Only what's done for Christ will last.

—C.T. Studd

I am grateful to have such loving, caring family and friends. You are my treasures. Actually, your involvement in my life has made *me* what I am. So if you don't like me, you are partly to blame. *"For none of us lives for ourselves alone, and none of us dies for ourselves alone"* (Romans 14:7, NIV).

During our lifetime, we are influenced by others and others are influenced by us. I trust that with God's help I have been able to contribute something positive into the lives of our family and friends. If I have any regrets, it would be that I could possibly have laid up more treasures in Heaven and done more for all of you whom I love and cherish.

I love you all and appreciate your love and care for us and for making me who I am…

"Me," Reubin.

My Life on the Homestead

Christmas Day on the Homestead

Christmas day on the homestead so many years ago;
Was just like every other day, yet very special though.
No decorated tree in the parlor with lights aglow.
There were a thousand trees outside covered with snow.

There was no room in the small log house
    for a Christmas tree.
Flashing lights were impossibility, without electricity,
We jumped quickly out of bed
    not to open Christmas gifts you see;
The cold room and floor made dressing in haste a necessity.

Still dark so the lantern was then lit,
    the morning chores to do.
Hay for the cows and horses, chickens grain,
    pigs got chop to chew,
After the cows were milked our breakfast
    was ready for us too.
Hot porridge, fresh milk, homemade bread
    with butter was our due.

After breakfast father would as always read
    a chapter from the Bible.
We were taught to listen with respect
    to God's word for it is reliable.
The Saviour born in a stable manger was indeed good news.
We knelt to pray, and give thanks
    that God's love for us we knew.

There were no gifts to open on Christmas day;
    only a brown candy bag.

The paper bag we got at the church celebration
  on Christmas night.
An orange, Cracker Jack popcorn box, a
  dinky toy, candy and nuts a few.
That Christmas bag brought more pleasure
  than a dozen gifts so new.

In our dire poverty small things brought us
  pleasure beyond measure.
We had so little and yet so much;
  family secure, God's love so pure.
Christmas day was filled with joy and peace
  because we knew for sure;
God showed His love for us;
  Jesus, Emmanuel, come to be our Saviour.

Christmas reminiscence of Reubin Drisner, 2009.

―

Welcome Danielle

The Drisner clan is a motley crew and very few.
We needed new recruits but what could we do?
So we commissioned Evan to search the world through.
To find someone special, someone new,
  not just anyone would do.

This person had to be special; this was Evan's commission.
She had to be beautiful with an even disposition.
She had to be intelligent and full of ambition.
Evan solemnly agreed to this supposition.

Evan diligently began his worldwide search.
He by serendipity found Danielle in a church.
With timidity and candor Evan began to pursue
This special girl he was sure she would do.

She was beautiful, intelligent, ambitious, and had a car too.
Wow! What else could he wish but to ask,
    "Will you say 'I DO'?"
We are proud to welcome you, Danielle, to the crew.
We are glad you are part of the family and We Love You.

Danielle, you're the first to get in;
    you're no different than kin.
Others will follow. Kyle is already out playing the field.
Kent may deny it but you can tell by his grin,
    it is easy to see.
But Danielle you're "Number 1";
    The Queen of the in-laws to be.

Welcome to the family, Danielle!

Compiled and read by Reubin Drisner at Evan & Danielle Drisner's wedding reception.

Welcome Sarah

Wow! Another addition to the Drisner Family Clan.
Blow the trumpets, beat the drums, clap your hands.
Kent had the courage to ask Sarah for his bride to be.
Congratulations Kent! Your choice is superb we can see.

"Sarah" meaning "Princess" was indeed chosen well.
A princess by birth and a princess by actions that tell.
Refined, kind, compassionate, and considerate of all.
Her beauty enhanced by quick wit and a mind on the ball.

Sarah's perception of Kent was that this avid sports fan,
Could be molded and changed to be a family man.
Sarah's task has begun after Kent said his "I DO."
With patience and candor her dream may come true.

Men are strange creatures who are quick to pursue,
But to change after marriage takes a lifetime to do.
Sarah, Kent is a gem in the rough; keep chipping away.
Your gem will appear before you are wrinkled and gray.

Kent, Sarah's three brothers are an awesome
    brigade of defense.
Don't mess with Sarah; treat her royally with common sense.
Sweet, gentle Sarah deserves the best and is now
    a part of the crew.
It's your task to make her life's dreams and wishes come true.

Sarah you're the second daughter-in-law but equal in kin.
We welcome you with joy and pride to the John Drisner den.
Your place in the family is sure and secure,
Your sweet disposition will enrich us all for sure.
Welcome to the Drisner Family, Sarah!

Composed for Kent and Sarah Drisner's wedding reception.

One of a Kind!

Ordinary things come in bunches, bags and bushels.
Cheaper by the dozen prepackaged and prepared.
But special things are chosen, hand-picked and unsoiled.
To become something extraordinary, one of a kind.

Nathaniel you are special with potential to refine.
You are a blessing, gifted with a big heart and keen mind.
A grandson better than you could be difficult to find.
We're proud you are in our family, close to our heart
    and mind.
You are one of a kind!

> *This is the day the Lord hath made,*
> *We will rejoice and be glad in it.*
> —Psalm 118:24

Happy Birthday, Nathaniel!
May your next year be abundantly blessed of God!

Epilogue

Reinhart and his wife Delores took over the homestead in 1959. Emil and Alvina, after twenty-eight years on the homestead, retired to Edmonton in a new house built by the family with lumber from the farm. For the rest of their lives they enjoyed the luxuries of urban living. The hard life on the homestead however took its toll. Alvina experienced a period of ill health and was finally put into a nursing home where shortly after that, at 71 years of age, she died of heart failure. Emil passed away in 1979 after several years of illness at the age of eighty.

Under Reinhart's farming skills, the farm prospered. More land was purchased. New farm equipment was bought. The farm was shifted from grain and dairy to a beef cattle ranch. Buildings were added as they were needed. Reinhart sold the farm in 1989 and had the largest farm sale in the history of that region. The new owners have turned the original homestead into a tree farm. The fields that we worked so hard to clear of trees now have straight rows of trees ready to be sold to landscapers. Farms in the region have been consolidated and turned into cattle ranches. The moonshiners couldn't compete with the liquor stores and hotels, so they shut down their stills. The Gamefield School was closed when school bussing was implemented. Years later the school was razed by a grass fire. The homesteaders' descendants have learned trades and left the farm to work elsewhere.

The new owners bulldozed the two-room log house we grew up in. The rest of the buildings are still all there. The stucco on the five-bedroom house we build in 1948 has been covered with white siding, which has made it look amazingly modern and new. The forest that was consumed by the 1936 fire that threatened to burn our house and barn, while the neighbours rallied to save the buildings, has grown back as big and dense as before. The clearing of the land and the drying up of some of the swamps has greatly reduced the mosquito, fly, gopher, and mice population. The trail through the bush will soon be a four-lane, paved, twinned highway to Fort McMurray.

Of the six siblings, only two of us, Ben and I, are left. We all succeeded in the various career choices we made. The next generation of descendants are educated and degreed. It is paradoxical that we, who had no teacher to teach us, now in the next generation have thirteen descendants who are classroom teachers and university/college professors.

Shirley and I have celebrated our sixtieth wedding anniversary. Sweet Shirley, ever-caring wife, mother, grandmother, and everybody's friend, unfortunately has been in hospitals for the past two years and is now in an extended health care facility. I'm now living in a comfortable, all-inclusive manor in Calgary that we thought Shirley and I would enjoy together. That, it now appears, will not happen. At eighty-five years of age, I feel my strength slowly seeping away. I am still mentally alert enough to know that my days are numbered. We don't know what the future holds, but from our homestead days we learned that God is only a prayer away. We are confident that the God of the homestead will be with us in the days to come. We also have the promise of the Lord that He gave us in the Gospel of John:

Do not let your hearts be troubled; trust in God; trust also in me. In my father's house are many rooms; if it were not so I would have told you. I am going to prepare a place for you. And if I go to prepare a place for you, I will come back and take you with me, that you may be where I am.

—John 14:1–3, NIV

—Reubin

Our children in 1991:
Clockwise from top L – Glenda, John, Sharon and Sandra

Some of the Emil Drisner descendants in Edmonton in 1986

My grandkids, 2007

CPSIA information can be obtained at www.ICGtesting.com
Printed in the USA
LVOW10s0901261114

415631LV00003B/14/P